This Book Belongs To:

____

____

Multiplying Fractions

1) $\frac{1}{2}$ x $\frac{3}{4}$ =   2) $\frac{1}{4}$ x $\frac{2}{3}$ =

3) $\frac{1}{2}$ x $\frac{1}{2}$ =   4) $\frac{2}{5}$ x $\frac{1}{2}$ =

5) $\frac{1}{3}$ x $\frac{2}{3}$ =   6) $\frac{2}{3}$ x $\frac{2}{5}$ =

7) $\frac{2}{3}$ x $\frac{1}{5}$ =   8) $\frac{3}{4}$ x $\frac{1}{2}$ =

9) $\frac{1}{3}$ x $\frac{1}{4}$ =   10) $\frac{1}{2}$ x $\frac{1}{2}$ =

11) $\frac{1}{2}$ x $\frac{3}{4}$ =   12) $\frac{4}{5}$ x $\frac{2}{3}$ =

13) $\frac{1}{5}$ x $\frac{4}{5}$ =   14) $\frac{1}{2}$ x $\frac{1}{3}$ =

15) $\frac{1}{3}$ x $\frac{2}{3}$ =   16) $\frac{2}{3}$ x $\frac{1}{4}$ =

17) $\frac{1}{2}$ x $\frac{1}{2}$ =   18) $\frac{3}{4}$ x $\frac{1}{2}$ =

19) $\frac{1}{2}$ x $\frac{1}{4}$ =   20) $\frac{1}{3}$ x $\frac{1}{2}$ =

21) $\frac{1}{2}$ x $\frac{3}{4}$ =   22) $\frac{3}{5}$ x $\frac{3}{4}$ =

23) $\frac{1}{2}$ x $\frac{1}{4}$ =   24) $\frac{1}{5}$ x $\frac{1}{2}$ =

25) $\frac{3}{4}$ x $\frac{1}{3}$ =   26) $\frac{4}{5}$ x $\frac{3}{4}$ =

27) $\frac{1}{4}$ x $\frac{1}{2}$ =   28) $\frac{1}{3}$ x $\frac{1}{4}$ =

29) $\frac{2}{5}$ x $\frac{1}{2}$ =   30) $\frac{2}{3}$ x $\frac{1}{2}$ =

1/62

1) $\frac{2}{5}$ x $\frac{1}{3}$ =

2) $\frac{1}{2}$ x $\frac{1}{4}$ =

3) $\frac{2}{5}$ x $\frac{2}{3}$ =

4) $\frac{3}{4}$ x $\frac{3}{4}$ =

5) $\frac{2}{3}$ x $\frac{1}{2}$ =

6) $\frac{1}{2}$ x $\frac{1}{3}$ =

7) $\frac{1}{3}$ x $\frac{1}{3}$ =

8) $\frac{1}{5}$ x $\frac{1}{4}$ =

9) $\frac{2}{5}$ x $\frac{1}{2}$ =

10) $\frac{2}{3}$ x $\frac{1}{2}$ =

11) $\frac{1}{3}$ x $\frac{1}{2}$ =

12) $\frac{1}{2}$ x $\frac{1}{3}$ =

13) $\frac{4}{5}$ x 1 =

14) $\frac{1}{3}$ x $\frac{3}{5}$ =

15) $\frac{1}{3}$ x $\frac{4}{5}$ =

16) $\frac{1}{4}$ x $\frac{1}{3}$ =

17) $\frac{3}{4}$ x $\frac{2}{3}$ =

18) $\frac{1}{2}$ x $\frac{1}{3}$ =

19) $\frac{1}{4}$ x $\frac{3}{4}$ =

20) $\frac{1}{2}$ x $\frac{1}{2}$ =

21) $\frac{1}{3}$ x $\frac{2}{3}$ =

22) $\frac{1}{3}$ x $\frac{1}{2}$ =

23) $\frac{3}{4}$ x $\frac{2}{3}$ =

24) $\frac{3}{5}$ x $\frac{2}{3}$ =

25) $\frac{1}{2}$ x $\frac{4}{5}$ =

26) $\frac{3}{4}$ x $\frac{1}{2}$ =

27) $\frac{2}{5}$ x $\frac{4}{5}$ =

28) $\frac{4}{5}$ x $\frac{1}{2}$ =

29) $\frac{1}{2}$ x $\frac{2}{3}$ =

30) $\frac{1}{3}$ x $\frac{3}{5}$ =

2/62

1) $\frac{1}{4}$ x $\frac{1}{2}$ =

2) $\frac{1}{5}$ x $\frac{3}{5}$ =

3) $\frac{3}{5}$ x $\frac{1}{5}$ =

4) $\frac{1}{2}$ x $\frac{1}{2}$ =

5) $\frac{1}{5}$ x $\frac{2}{3}$ =

6) $\frac{1}{3}$ x $\frac{1}{2}$ =

7) $\frac{2}{3}$ x $\frac{3}{4}$ =

8) $\frac{1}{2}$ x $\frac{1}{3}$ =

9) $\frac{1}{4}$ x 1 =

10) $\frac{2}{3}$ x $\frac{1}{2}$ =

11) $\frac{1}{3}$ x $\frac{4}{5}$ =

12) 1 x $\frac{1}{3}$ =

13) $\frac{2}{5}$ x $\frac{2}{5}$ =

14) $\frac{1}{2}$ x $\frac{1}{3}$ =

15) $\frac{2}{3}$ x $\frac{2}{3}$ =

16) $\frac{1}{2}$ x $\frac{2}{3}$ =

17) 1 x $\frac{3}{4}$ =

18) $\frac{1}{4}$ x $\frac{1}{2}$ =

19) $\frac{1}{2}$ x $\frac{3}{4}$ =

20) $\frac{4}{5}$ x $\frac{1}{3}$ =

21) $\frac{4}{5}$ x $\frac{3}{5}$ =

22) $\frac{3}{4}$ x $\frac{2}{5}$ =

23) $\frac{1}{3}$ x $\frac{1}{2}$ =

24) $\frac{1}{2}$ x $\frac{3}{4}$ =

25) $\frac{3}{4}$ x $\frac{1}{2}$ =

26) $\frac{1}{2}$ x $\frac{1}{2}$ =

27) 1 x $\frac{3}{5}$ =

28) $\frac{1}{2}$ x $\frac{1}{4}$ =

29) $\frac{4}{5}$ x $\frac{1}{2}$ =

30) $\frac{2}{3}$ x $\frac{3}{4}$ =

3/62

1) $\frac{1}{2}$ x $\frac{2}{3}$ =

2) $\frac{3}{5}$ x $\frac{3}{5}$ =

3) $\frac{1}{3}$ x $\frac{2}{3}$ =

4) $\frac{2}{3}$ x $\frac{3}{5}$ =

5) $\frac{4}{5}$ x $\frac{2}{5}$ =

6) $\frac{1}{3}$ x $\frac{1}{2}$ =

7) $\frac{1}{2}$ x $\frac{1}{3}$ =

8) $\frac{1}{3}$ x 1 =

9) $\frac{1}{2}$ x $\frac{3}{4}$ =

10) $\frac{1}{4}$ x $\frac{1}{2}$ =

11) $\frac{1}{3}$ x $\frac{1}{2}$ =

12) $\frac{1}{2}$ x $\frac{4}{5}$ =

13) $\frac{3}{5}$ x $\frac{2}{3}$ =

14) $\frac{3}{4}$ x $\frac{2}{3}$ =

15) $\frac{1}{2}$ x $\frac{1}{4}$ =

4/62

16) $\frac{1}{4}$ x $\frac{3}{4}$ =

17) $\frac{1}{2}$ x $\frac{1}{3}$ =

18) $\frac{3}{5}$ x $\frac{1}{3}$ =

19) $\frac{1}{2}$ x $\frac{3}{5}$ =

20) $\frac{2}{3}$ x $\frac{1}{2}$ =

21) $\frac{1}{2}$ x $\frac{1}{2}$ =

22) $\frac{2}{3}$ x $\frac{1}{2}$ =

23) $\frac{2}{3}$ x $\frac{2}{5}$ =

24) $\frac{3}{4}$ x $\frac{3}{4}$ =

25) $\frac{1}{2}$ x $\frac{2}{5}$ =

26) $\frac{2}{5}$ x $\frac{1}{3}$ =

27) $\frac{1}{3}$ x $\frac{3}{4}$ =

28) $\frac{1}{2}$ x $\frac{1}{2}$ =

29) $\frac{1}{5}$ x $\frac{1}{3}$ =

30) $\frac{1}{5}$ x $\frac{3}{5}$ =

1) $\frac{1}{2} \times \frac{1}{5} =$ 2) $\frac{3}{4} \times \frac{1}{3} =$

3) $\frac{1}{2} \times \frac{2}{3} =$ 4) $\frac{1}{2} \times \frac{3}{5} =$

5) $\frac{2}{3} \times \frac{1}{2} =$ 6) $\frac{3}{4} \times \frac{1}{2} =$

7) $\frac{1}{3} \times \frac{2}{3} =$ 8) $\frac{4}{5} \times \frac{2}{3} =$

9) $\frac{1}{5} \times \frac{1}{5} =$ 10) $\frac{3}{4} \times \frac{1}{2} =$

11) $\frac{2}{5} \times \frac{2}{3} =$ 12) $\frac{3}{4} \times \frac{1}{2} =$

13) $\frac{3}{5} \times \frac{2}{5} =$ 14) $\frac{3}{5} \times \frac{1}{2} =$

5/62

15) $\frac{1}{3} \times \frac{2}{3} =$ 16) $\frac{1}{2} \times \frac{3}{5} =$

17) $\frac{2}{3} \times \frac{2}{3} =$ 18) $\frac{2}{3} \times \frac{4}{5} =$

19) $\frac{1}{3} \times \frac{1}{2} =$ 20) $\frac{1}{4} \times \frac{1}{3} =$

21) $\frac{1}{2} \times \frac{3}{4} =$ 22) $\frac{1}{5} \times \frac{1}{5} =$

23) $\frac{1}{4} \times \frac{3}{5} =$ 24) $\frac{2}{5} \times \frac{1}{5} =$

25) $\frac{3}{5} \times 1 =$ 26) $\frac{3}{4} \times \frac{3}{4} =$

27) $\frac{1}{3} \times \frac{1}{5} =$ 28) $\frac{1}{2} \times \frac{4}{5} =$

29) $\frac{1}{2} \times \frac{1}{4} =$ 30) $\frac{1}{3} \times \frac{1}{2} =$

1) $\frac{1}{5} \times \frac{4}{3} =$

2) $\frac{13}{7} \times \frac{11}{3} =$

3) $4 \times \frac{1}{3} =$

4) $\frac{10}{7} \times 2 =$

5) $\frac{4}{5} \times \frac{3}{2} =$

6) $\frac{8}{7} \times \frac{9}{2} =$

7) $2 \times \frac{2}{3} =$

8) $\frac{21}{8} \times 1 =$

9) $\frac{6}{5} \times 3 =$

10) $\frac{11}{4} \times \frac{7}{3} =$

11) $\frac{35}{8} \times 4 =$

12) $\frac{1}{4} \times \frac{9}{2} =$

13) $\frac{3}{2} \times 2 =$

14) $\frac{4}{3} \times \frac{9}{2} =$

15) $\frac{3}{4} \times \frac{5}{2} =$

16) $\frac{9}{2} \times \frac{5}{4} =$

17) $\frac{3}{7} \times 2 =$

18) $\frac{13}{5} \times \frac{9}{2} =$

19) $1 \times \frac{4}{3} =$

20) $\frac{7}{2} \times \frac{9}{2} =$

21) $\frac{9}{4} \times \frac{15}{4} =$

22) $\frac{11}{5} \times \frac{5}{4} =$

23) $\frac{13}{5} \times \frac{9}{2} =$

24) $\frac{29}{6} \times \frac{1}{5} =$

25) $\frac{23}{6} \times \frac{7}{3} =$

26) $\frac{5}{2} \times \frac{19}{5} =$

27) $2 \times \frac{5}{2} =$

28) $\frac{1}{2} \times \frac{2}{5} =$

29) $4 \times \frac{9}{2} =$

30) $\frac{25}{6} \times \frac{13}{5} =$

1) $\frac{19}{7} \times \frac{11}{4} =$

2) $\frac{11}{4} \times \frac{11}{3} =$

3) $4 \times \frac{24}{5} =$

4) $\frac{24}{5} \times 5 =$

5) $\frac{5}{2} \times \frac{4}{3} =$

6) $\frac{19}{4} \times 5 =$

7) $\frac{3}{2} \times 4 =$

8) $\frac{2}{5} \times 4 =$

9) $\frac{16}{5} \times \frac{4}{3} =$

10) $\frac{1}{3} \times 2 =$

11) $\frac{10}{7} \times \frac{13}{5} =$

12) $\frac{26}{7} \times 3 =$

13) $\frac{21}{5} \times \frac{1}{2} =$

14) $\frac{17}{4} \times \frac{7}{5} =$

15) $\frac{1}{4} \times \frac{23}{5} =$

16) $\frac{3}{7} \times 1 =$

17) $\frac{34}{7} \times \frac{13}{3} =$

18) $\frac{13}{4} \times 4 =$

19) $\frac{7}{2} \times 2 =$

20) $\frac{7}{6} \times \frac{15}{4} =$

21) $5 \times \frac{2}{3} =$

22) $\frac{27}{7} \times \frac{1}{4} =$

23) $\frac{13}{3} \times \frac{23}{5} =$

24) $5 \times \frac{3}{4} =$

25) $5 \times \frac{14}{3} =$

26) $\frac{13}{5} \times \frac{7}{2} =$

27) $\frac{3}{4} \times \frac{4}{5} =$

28) $\frac{31}{7} \times \frac{14}{3} =$

29) $\frac{21}{5} \times \frac{7}{3} =$

30) $\frac{1}{2} \times 2 =$

7/62

1) $\frac{3}{4}$ x 5 =

2) $\frac{5}{2}$ x $\frac{10}{3}$ =

3) $\frac{8}{7}$ x $\frac{22}{5}$ =

4) $\frac{9}{4}$ x $\frac{9}{2}$ =

5) $\frac{19}{7}$ x $\frac{14}{5}$ =

6) $\frac{21}{5}$ x $\frac{13}{4}$ =

7) $\frac{17}{4}$ x $\frac{13}{3}$ =

8) $\frac{5}{2}$ x $\frac{4}{3}$ =

9) $\frac{39}{8}$ x $\frac{6}{5}$ =

10) $\frac{22}{5}$ x $\frac{7}{3}$ =

11) $\frac{13}{3}$ x 4 =

12) $\frac{9}{8}$ x 2 =

13) $\frac{8}{3}$ x $\frac{2}{3}$ =

14) $\frac{4}{3}$ x $\frac{2}{3}$ =

15) $\frac{5}{2}$ x $\frac{4}{3}$ =

16) $\frac{7}{4}$ x $\frac{18}{5}$ =

17) $\frac{16}{5}$ x $\frac{16}{3}$ =

18) $\frac{3}{7}$ x $\frac{5}{4}$ =

19) 1 x $\frac{13}{3}$ =

20) $\frac{9}{4}$ x $\frac{9}{2}$ =

21) $\frac{9}{4}$ x 3 =

22) $\frac{13}{4}$ x $\frac{5}{4}$ =

23) $\frac{17}{6}$ x 5 =

24) 2 x $\frac{2}{3}$ =

25) $\frac{7}{2}$ x $\frac{11}{4}$ =

26) $\frac{1}{2}$ x 2 =

27) 4 x $\frac{2}{3}$ =

28) $\frac{9}{2}$ x $\frac{23}{5}$ =

29) $\frac{3}{2}$ x $\frac{3}{4}$ =

30) $\frac{32}{7}$ x 1 =

8/62

1) $\frac{8}{3} \times \frac{13}{5} =$

2) $\frac{9}{2} \times \frac{23}{5} =$

3) $\frac{7}{2} \times 5 =$

4) $\frac{6}{5} \times \frac{5}{2} =$

5) $\frac{3}{7} \times 3 =$

6) $\frac{15}{4} \times \frac{8}{5} =$

7) $\frac{2}{3} \times 4 =$

8) $\frac{7}{2} \times \frac{7}{3} =$

9) $\frac{4}{3} \times \frac{5}{2} =$

10) $\frac{1}{2} \times \frac{9}{2} =$

11) $\frac{9}{2} \times 5 =$

12) $\frac{17}{7} \times \frac{1}{3} =$

13) $\frac{5}{2} \times \frac{3}{5} =$

14) $\frac{6}{5} \times \frac{13}{3} =$

15) $3 \times \frac{1}{3} =$

16) $\frac{22}{7} \times \frac{4}{3} =$

17) $\frac{3}{2} \times \frac{5}{2} =$

18) $\frac{1}{4} \times 1 =$

19) $\frac{22}{7} \times \frac{11}{2} =$

20) $\frac{17}{4} \times \frac{3}{2} =$

21) $\frac{11}{2} \times \frac{9}{2} =$

22) $\frac{13}{6} \times 3 =$

23) $\frac{11}{3} \times 4 =$

24) $\frac{7}{2} \times \frac{5}{2} =$

25) $3 \times \frac{2}{3} =$

26) $\frac{24}{7} \times \frac{13}{5} =$

27) $\frac{11}{2} \times \frac{16}{3} =$

28) $\frac{16}{7} \times \frac{15}{4} =$

29) $\frac{10}{3} \times \frac{3}{2} =$

30) $3 \times \frac{13}{4} =$

9/62

1) $\frac{11}{3} \times \frac{3}{4} =$

2) $\frac{2}{3} \times \frac{9}{2} =$

3) $5 \times \frac{5}{4} =$

4) $\frac{7}{3} \times \frac{4}{3} =$

5) $\frac{17}{5} \times \frac{9}{2} =$

6) $\frac{35}{8} \times \frac{12}{5} =$

7) $\frac{4}{3} \times \frac{12}{5} =$

8) $\frac{13}{3} \times \frac{11}{5} =$

9) $3 \times \frac{7}{2} =$

10) $\frac{3}{8} \times \frac{9}{2} =$

11) $\frac{5}{4} \times 4 =$

12) $\frac{3}{2} \times \frac{1}{2} =$

13) $2 \times \frac{9}{2} =$

14) $\frac{5}{8} \times 2 =$

15) $\frac{1}{2} \times 5 =$

16) $\frac{1}{8} \times \frac{1}{2} =$

17) $\frac{17}{4} \times \frac{11}{2} =$

18) $\frac{9}{2} \times 3 =$

19) $\frac{18}{5} \times \frac{9}{4} =$

20) $\frac{26}{7} \times 1 =$

21) $\frac{2}{3} \times 1 =$

22) $\frac{31}{6} \times \frac{7}{2} =$

23) $\frac{14}{3} \times \frac{11}{5} =$

24) $\frac{1}{3} \times \frac{3}{4} =$

25) $\frac{1}{3} \times \frac{7}{4} =$

26) $\frac{9}{8} \times 5 =$

27) $\frac{19}{5} \times 1 =$

28) $\frac{4}{3} \times \frac{3}{5} =$

29) $\frac{5}{2} \times \frac{11}{4} =$

30) $\frac{17}{7} \times \frac{2}{3} =$

1) $\frac{16}{5} \times \frac{17}{4} =$

2) $\frac{7}{4} \times \frac{1}{2} =$

3) $\frac{10}{3} \times \frac{4}{3} =$

4) $\frac{1}{4} \times 5 =$

5) $\frac{2}{7} \times \frac{17}{4} =$

6) $\frac{15}{7} \times \frac{13}{5} =$

7) $\frac{7}{4} \times \frac{5}{2} =$

8) $\frac{4}{3} \times \frac{2}{3} =$

9) $\frac{11}{4} \times \frac{18}{5} =$

10) $\frac{9}{2} \times 5 =$

11) $5 \times \frac{11}{5} =$

12) $\frac{5}{2} \times 3 =$

13) $\frac{2}{3} \times \frac{14}{3} =$

14) $\frac{7}{3} \times 3 =$

15) $\frac{10}{3} \times 1 =$

11/62

16) $\frac{7}{3} \times \frac{8}{3} =$

17) $5 \times \frac{3}{4} =$

18) $\frac{2}{3} \times \frac{1}{2} =$

19) $\frac{17}{4} \times \frac{7}{3} =$

20) $\frac{6}{5} \times \frac{9}{2} =$

21) $\frac{20}{7} \times 1 =$

22) $\frac{13}{8} \times 5 =$

23) $\frac{13}{4} \times 5 =$

24) $5 \times \frac{11}{3} =$

25) $4 \times \frac{11}{3} =$

26) $\frac{1}{3} \times \frac{15}{4} =$

27) $5 \times \frac{2}{3} =$

28) $\frac{26}{7} \times \frac{12}{5} =$

29) $\frac{3}{5} \times \frac{3}{2} =$

30) $3 \times \frac{2}{3} =$

1) $\frac{1}{6} \times \frac{5}{2} =$

2) $\frac{39}{8} \times \frac{1}{2} =$

3) $\frac{19}{8} \times \frac{10}{3} =$

4) $\frac{3}{2} \times 5 =$

5) $\frac{10}{3} \times 3 =$

6) $\frac{7}{4} \times \frac{3}{2} =$

7) $1 \times \frac{4}{3} =$

8) $\frac{17}{7} \times \frac{7}{2} =$

9) $\frac{5}{4} \times \frac{3}{2} =$

10) $2 \times \frac{1}{3} =$

11) $4 \times \frac{2}{5} =$

12) $2 \times \frac{10}{3} =$

13) $4 \times \frac{5}{3} =$

14) $4 \times \frac{3}{2} =$

15) $3 \times \frac{1}{3} =$

16) $\frac{12}{5} \times 4 =$

17) $\frac{4}{5} \times 1 =$

18) $2 \times \frac{19}{5} =$

19) $\frac{27}{7} \times \frac{19}{5} =$

20) $3 \times \frac{5}{2} =$

21) $\frac{29}{7} \times \frac{5}{2} =$

22) $\frac{16}{5} \times 4 =$

23) $\frac{26}{7} \times 1 =$

24) $\frac{5}{2} \times 4 =$

25) $\frac{7}{8} \times 1 =$

26) $\frac{6}{7} \times \frac{1}{3} =$

27) $\frac{1}{7} \times \frac{13}{3} =$

28) $\frac{11}{3} \times \frac{5}{2} =$

29) $\frac{19}{7} \times \frac{9}{2} =$

30) $\frac{11}{5} \times \frac{3}{4} =$

12/62

1) $\frac{21}{8} \times \frac{18}{5} =$

2) $\frac{18}{7} \times 3 =$

3) $\frac{1}{2} \times \frac{7}{2} =$

4) $\frac{32}{7} \times 2 =$

5) $\frac{23}{6} \times \frac{7}{2} =$

6) $\frac{18}{5} \times 3 =$

7) $\frac{13}{3} \times \frac{15}{4} =$

8) $1 \times \frac{3}{2} =$

9) $\frac{17}{6} \times \frac{1}{2} =$

10) $\frac{33}{7} \times \frac{18}{5} =$

11) $\frac{4}{3} \times \frac{17}{4} =$

12) $3 \times \frac{12}{5} =$

13) $\frac{8}{5} \times 2 =$

14) $\frac{11}{4} \times \frac{10}{3} =$

15) $\frac{8}{7} \times \frac{6}{5} =$

16) $\frac{5}{4} \times \frac{1}{4} =$

17) $\frac{21}{5} \times 1 =$

18) $\frac{11}{8} \times 1 =$

19) $3 \times \frac{15}{4} =$

20) $\frac{17}{5} \times \frac{17}{4} =$

21) $1 \times \frac{7}{3} =$

22) $\frac{9}{2} \times 2 =$

23) $\frac{17}{4} \times \frac{5}{4} =$

24) $\frac{7}{2} \times 1 =$

25) $\frac{11}{4} \times \frac{16}{5} =$

26) $\frac{3}{2} \times \frac{9}{2} =$

27) $\frac{7}{3} \times 3 =$

28) $\frac{23}{5} \times \frac{5}{3} =$

29) $\frac{3}{2} \times \frac{13}{5} =$

30) $\frac{9}{4} \times 5 =$

13/62

1) $\frac{1}{8} \times 1 =$

2) $\frac{4}{5} \times \frac{13}{4} =$

3) $\frac{19}{8} \times 3 =$

4) $\frac{1}{4} \times \frac{5}{2} =$

5) $\frac{6}{5} \times \frac{8}{5} =$

6) $\frac{7}{6} \times 3 =$

7) $2 \times \frac{11}{3} =$

8) $\frac{1}{5} \times \frac{19}{4} =$

9) $\frac{5}{2} \times 1 =$

10) $\frac{19}{4} \times 2 =$

11) $\frac{19}{10} \times \frac{5}{2} =$

12) $\frac{8}{3} \times \frac{10}{3} =$

13) $\frac{13}{4} \times 4 =$

14) $\frac{5}{9} \times \frac{3}{4} =$

15) $\frac{3}{5} \times \frac{5}{2} =$

16) $\frac{18}{5} \times 2 =$

17) $3 \times \frac{3}{2} =$

18) $\frac{8}{5} \times \frac{9}{2} =$

19) $\frac{15}{8} \times 4 =$

20) $\frac{11}{5} \times \frac{7}{3} =$

21) $\frac{7}{8} \times \frac{3}{2} =$

22) $2 \times \frac{13}{4} =$

23) $\frac{13}{6} \times \frac{19}{5} =$

24) $\frac{3}{2} \times \frac{13}{4} =$

25) $\frac{7}{5} \times \frac{9}{4} =$

26) $\frac{15}{8} \times 1 =$

27) $\frac{7}{3} \times 5 =$

28) $\frac{11}{6} \times 3 =$

29) $\frac{7}{2} \times \frac{16}{5} =$

30) $\frac{7}{2} \times \frac{7}{2} =$

14/62

1) $\frac{19}{5}$ x $\frac{14}{3}$ =   2) $\frac{15}{8}$ x $\frac{3}{2}$ =

3) $\frac{11}{3}$ x $\frac{1}{2}$ =   4) $\frac{14}{5}$ x 2 =

5) $\frac{1}{2}$ x $\frac{8}{3}$ =   6) $\frac{5}{3}$ x $\frac{1}{3}$ =

7) $\frac{41}{10}$ x 2 =   8) $\frac{24}{7}$ x 5 =

9) $\frac{16}{5}$ x $\frac{1}{5}$ =   10) $\frac{5}{3}$ x $\frac{18}{5}$ =

11) $\frac{5}{4}$ x $\frac{5}{2}$ =   12) $\frac{2}{3}$ x $\frac{8}{3}$ =

13) $\frac{22}{7}$ x $\frac{13}{3}$ =   14) $\frac{10}{3}$ x $\frac{1}{5}$ =

15) $\frac{7}{2}$ x $\frac{13}{3}$ =   **15/62**   16) $\frac{14}{5}$ x $\frac{3}{2}$ =

17) $\frac{7}{8}$ x $\frac{1}{5}$ =   18) $\frac{11}{7}$ x $\frac{2}{3}$ =

19) $\frac{4}{3}$ x $\frac{1}{2}$ =   20) $\frac{31}{7}$ x $\frac{5}{4}$ =

21) $\frac{7}{3}$ x $\frac{13}{4}$ =   22) $\frac{13}{7}$ x $\frac{16}{5}$ =

23) $\frac{29}{7}$ x $\frac{7}{2}$ =   24) $\frac{15}{4}$ x 3 =

25) $\frac{13}{4}$ x $\frac{14}{3}$ =   26) $\frac{20}{9}$ x 4 =

27) $\frac{3}{2}$ x $\frac{11}{4}$ =   28) $\frac{5}{4}$ x $\frac{9}{2}$ =

29) $\frac{2}{3}$ x 3 =   30) $\frac{11}{5}$ x 2 =

1) $3 \times \frac{7}{2} =$

2) $\frac{2}{5} \times 2 =$

3) $\frac{3}{2} \times \frac{5}{2} =$

4) $5 \times \frac{3}{2} =$

5) $\frac{1}{2} \times \frac{7}{3} =$

6) $\frac{30}{7} \times 2 =$

7) $\frac{16}{7} \times \frac{1}{2} =$

8) $4 \times \frac{2}{3} =$

9) $\frac{9}{8} \times 4 =$

10) $\frac{8}{3} \times 4 =$

11) $\frac{8}{3} \times \frac{19}{5} =$

12) $3 \times \frac{12}{5} =$

13) $4 \times \frac{1}{2} =$

14) $\frac{24}{5} \times 3 =$

15) $\frac{22}{5} \times \frac{9}{5} =$

16/62

16) $3 \times \frac{11}{4} =$

17) $\frac{35}{9} \times 1 =$

18) $\frac{15}{4} \times \frac{1}{2} =$

19) $\frac{16}{7} \times \frac{22}{5} =$

20) $3 \times \frac{17}{4} =$

21) $\frac{7}{2} \times \frac{5}{3} =$

22) $\frac{9}{10} \times 2 =$

23) $\frac{5}{2} \times \frac{1}{2} =$

24) $\frac{3}{2} \times \frac{9}{2} =$

25) $\frac{5}{3} \times 4 =$

26) $\frac{33}{7} \times \frac{5}{2} =$

27) $\frac{17}{4} \times 5 =$

28) $\frac{35}{8} \times \frac{10}{3} =$

29) $\frac{39}{8} \times 3 =$

30) $\frac{22}{5} \times \frac{18}{5} =$

1) $\frac{25}{8}$ x $\frac{16}{5}$ =

2) $\frac{10}{7}$ x $\frac{14}{3}$ =

3) $\frac{8}{9}$ x $\frac{19}{5}$ =

4) 4 x $\frac{11}{4}$ =

5) $\frac{21}{5}$ x 3 =

6) $\frac{17}{5}$ x $\frac{7}{2}$ =

7) $\frac{19}{4}$ x 3 =

8) $\frac{1}{3}$ x 3 =

9) 1 x $\frac{17}{4}$ =

10) $\frac{24}{5}$ x $\frac{1}{5}$ =

11) $\frac{5}{3}$ x 2 =

12) 3 x $\frac{1}{2}$ =

13) $\frac{30}{7}$ x $\frac{14}{5}$ =

14) $\frac{19}{4}$ x $\frac{5}{2}$ =

15) 2 x $\frac{17}{4}$ =

17/62

16) $\frac{16}{9}$ x $\frac{9}{2}$ =

17) $\frac{12}{5}$ x $\frac{5}{3}$ =

18) $\frac{8}{3}$ x 3 =

19) 4 x $\frac{3}{2}$ =

20) $\frac{21}{5}$ x $\frac{9}{2}$ =

21) $\frac{11}{3}$ x $\frac{9}{5}$ =

22) $\frac{35}{8}$ x $\frac{1}{3}$ =

23) $\frac{9}{2}$ x $\frac{1}{3}$ =

24) $\frac{1}{9}$ x 2 =

25) $\frac{1}{6}$ x 4 =

26) $\frac{1}{2}$ x $\frac{1}{2}$ =

27) $\frac{4}{5}$ x $\frac{5}{3}$ =

28) $\frac{9}{2}$ x 3 =

29) $\frac{27}{8}$ x $\frac{7}{2}$ =

30) $\frac{3}{5}$ x 5 =

1) $\frac{7}{10} \times \frac{7}{2} =$

2) $\frac{11}{3} \times \frac{7}{3} =$

3) $\frac{19}{4} \times \frac{13}{3} =$

4) $\frac{10}{9} \times 1 =$

5) $\frac{22}{5} \times \frac{14}{5} =$

6) $\frac{3}{2} \times \frac{9}{2} =$

7) $\frac{1}{3} \times \frac{18}{5} =$

8) $\frac{19}{10} \times \frac{13}{3} =$

9) $\frac{15}{4} \times \frac{4}{3} =$

10) $\frac{32}{9} \times \frac{2}{3} =$

11) $\frac{4}{3} \times 3 =$

12) $1 \times \frac{19}{5} =$

13) $\frac{38}{9} \times 1 =$

14) $\frac{11}{9} \times 4 =$

15) $\frac{3}{2} \times \frac{5}{2} =$

18/62

16) $\frac{11}{4} \times 1 =$

17) $4 \times \frac{4}{3} =$

18) $1 \times \frac{14}{3} =$

19) $\frac{4}{9} \times \frac{3}{2} =$

20) $\frac{3}{2} \times \frac{10}{3} =$

21) $5 \times \frac{10}{3} =$

22) $1 \times \frac{4}{3} =$

23) $\frac{2}{5} \times \frac{22}{5} =$

24) $1 \times \frac{5}{2} =$

25) $\frac{5}{4} \times \frac{9}{2} =$

26) $\frac{4}{5} \times 3 =$

27) $\frac{15}{4} \times 5 =$

28) $\frac{10}{3} \times \frac{22}{5} =$

29) $\frac{11}{9} \times \frac{21}{5} =$

30) $\frac{19}{4} \times 2 =$

1) $2 \times \frac{5}{4} =$

2) $\frac{5}{3} \times \frac{17}{5} =$

3) $\frac{13}{4} \times \frac{13}{4} =$

4) $\frac{18}{7} \times \frac{2}{3} =$

5) $\frac{1}{6} \times \frac{6}{5} =$

6) $\frac{5}{2} \times \frac{3}{5} =$

7) $\frac{6}{5} \times \frac{10}{3} =$

8) $\frac{10}{3} \times \frac{1}{2} =$

9) $\frac{5}{3} \times \frac{3}{2} =$

10) $\frac{6}{7} \times 2 =$

11) $1 \times \frac{13}{5} =$

12) $\frac{13}{5} \times \frac{11}{3} =$

13) $\frac{18}{5} \times \frac{19}{4} =$

14) $\frac{11}{8} \times \frac{11}{4} =$

15) $\frac{29}{7} \times \frac{7}{2} =$

19/62

16) $\frac{6}{7} \times \frac{9}{4} =$

17) $1 \times \frac{17}{4} =$

18) $\frac{23}{5} \times 1 =$

19) $\frac{7}{3} \times \frac{9}{2} =$

20) $\frac{35}{9} \times \frac{1}{2} =$

21) $\frac{1}{6} \times \frac{22}{5} =$

22) $\frac{4}{7} \times \frac{3}{4} =$

23) $\frac{2}{5} \times 1 =$

24) $\frac{9}{4} \times \frac{11}{3} =$

25) $\frac{11}{3} \times 4 =$

26) $\frac{13}{3} \times \frac{1}{2} =$

27) $\frac{1}{2} \times \frac{12}{5} =$

28) $5 \times \frac{1}{4} =$

29) $\frac{10}{7} \times \frac{7}{2} =$

30) $\frac{7}{8} \times \frac{5}{3} =$

1) $\frac{27}{8} \times 1 =$

2) $\frac{9}{2} \times \frac{21}{5} =$

3) $\frac{31}{9} \times \frac{7}{5} =$

4) $\frac{9}{2} \times \frac{6}{5} =$

5) $\frac{8}{3} \times \frac{9}{2} =$

6) $4 \times \frac{19}{4} =$

7) $\frac{7}{10} \times \frac{10}{3} =$

8) $\frac{29}{10} \times \frac{5}{2} =$

9) $\frac{39}{10} \times \frac{11}{3} =$

10) $\frac{1}{5} \times \frac{3}{2} =$

11) $4 \times \frac{11}{3} =$

12) $\frac{32}{7} \times \frac{7}{2} =$

13) $\frac{1}{5} \times \frac{9}{2} =$

14) $\frac{7}{10} \times \frac{7}{2} =$

15) $3 \times \frac{7}{4} =$

16) $\frac{3}{2} \times 3 =$

20/62

17) $\frac{22}{5} \times \frac{4}{3} =$

18) $\frac{19}{6} \times \frac{9}{4} =$

19) $\frac{30}{7} \times \frac{5}{2} =$

20) $\frac{37}{10} \times \frac{13}{3} =$

21) $\frac{4}{3} \times 3 =$

22) $\frac{7}{2} \times \frac{5}{4} =$

23) $\frac{7}{6} \times \frac{19}{5} =$

24) $4 \times \frac{1}{2} =$

25) $\frac{23}{9} \times 3 =$

26) $\frac{7}{2} \times \frac{5}{4} =$

27) $\frac{5}{2} \times 5 =$

28) $\frac{9}{4} \times \frac{5}{2} =$

29) $\frac{9}{2} \times \frac{4}{3} =$

30) $\frac{7}{3} \times 4 =$

Dividing Fractions

1) $\frac{2}{5} \div \frac{1}{5} =$

2) $\frac{1}{2} \div \frac{1}{2} =$

3) $\frac{2}{5} \div \frac{5}{7} =$

4) $\frac{3}{5} \div \frac{1}{2} =$

5) $\frac{2}{3} \div \frac{3}{4} =$

6) $\frac{1}{2} \div \frac{1}{2} =$

7) $\frac{3}{4} \div \frac{1}{3} =$

8) $\frac{1}{3} \div \frac{1}{7} =$

9) $\frac{1}{2} \div \frac{6}{7} =$

10) $\frac{1}{2} \div 1 =$

11) $\frac{3}{4} \div \frac{2}{5} =$

12) $\frac{4}{5} \div \frac{3}{7} =$

13) $\frac{1}{4} \div \frac{1}{2} =$

14) $\frac{1}{2} \div \frac{1}{2} =$

21/62

15) $\frac{1}{3} \div \frac{5}{7} =$

16) $\frac{1}{3} \div \frac{4}{5} =$

17) $\frac{1}{2} \div \frac{3}{5} =$

18) $\frac{1}{3} \div \frac{1}{2} =$

19) $\frac{1}{2} \div \frac{4}{7} =$

20) $\frac{4}{5} \div \frac{7}{8} =$

21) $\frac{1}{2} \div \frac{4}{5} =$

22) $\frac{1}{3} \div \frac{1}{3} =$

23) $\frac{3}{4} \div \frac{3}{8} =$

24) $\frac{1}{2} \div \frac{5}{8} =$

25) $\frac{1}{2} \div \frac{1}{3} =$

26) $\frac{4}{5} \div \frac{1}{4} =$

27) $\frac{1}{2} \div \frac{1}{4} =$

28) $\frac{3}{5} \div \frac{4}{5} =$

29) $\frac{1}{2} \div \frac{3}{5} =$

30) $\frac{1}{2} \div \frac{6}{7} =$

1) $\frac{2}{3} \div \frac{1}{2} =$

2) $\frac{1}{2} \div \frac{1}{5} =$

3) $\frac{1}{2} \div \frac{7}{8} =$

4) $\frac{2}{3} \div \frac{5}{8} =$

5) $\frac{1}{2} \div \frac{3}{5} =$

6) $1 \div \frac{7}{8} =$

7) $\frac{3}{4} \div \frac{1}{7} =$

8) $\frac{3}{4} \div \frac{3}{8} =$

9) $\frac{1}{2} \div \frac{6}{7} =$

10) $\frac{2}{5} \div \frac{1}{7} =$

11) $\frac{3}{5} \div \frac{1}{4} =$

12) $\frac{1}{2} \div \frac{1}{2} =$

13) $\frac{3}{5} \div \frac{2}{3} =$

14) $\frac{1}{2} \div \frac{1}{2} =$

15) $\frac{1}{5} \div \frac{4}{7} =$

22/62

16) $\frac{1}{2} \div \frac{1}{4} =$

17) $\frac{1}{2} \div \frac{2}{3} =$

18) $\frac{2}{3} \div \frac{1}{4} =$

19) $\frac{1}{3} \div \frac{4}{7} =$

20) $\frac{1}{2} \div \frac{1}{8} =$

21) $\frac{1}{4} \div \frac{3}{4} =$

22) $\frac{1}{2} \div \frac{1}{2} =$

23) $\frac{3}{4} \div \frac{1}{2} =$

24) $\frac{2}{3} \div \frac{4}{5} =$

25) $\frac{1}{2} \div \frac{5}{7} =$

26) $\frac{1}{2} \div \frac{1}{2} =$

27) $\frac{1}{2} \div \frac{7}{8} =$

28) $\frac{1}{2} \div \frac{3}{8} =$

29) $\frac{3}{4} \div \frac{1}{2} =$

30) $\frac{2}{3} \div \frac{1}{2} =$

1) $\frac{1}{3} \div \frac{2}{3} =$

2) $\frac{1}{2} \div \frac{5}{7} =$

3) $\frac{1}{5} \div \frac{1}{3} =$

4) $\frac{1}{2} \div \frac{1}{2} =$

5) $\frac{2}{5} \div \frac{1}{2} =$

6) $\frac{1}{2} \div \frac{5}{6} =$

7) $\frac{3}{5} \div \frac{1}{7} =$

8) $\frac{1}{3} \div \frac{3}{4} =$

9) $\frac{1}{2} \div \frac{1}{4} =$

10) $\frac{3}{5} \div \frac{4}{7} =$

11) $\frac{3}{5} \div \frac{1}{3} =$

12) $\frac{3}{4} \div \frac{1}{2} =$

13) $\frac{1}{3} \div \frac{1}{3} =$

14) $\frac{1}{2} \div \frac{6}{7} =$

15) $\frac{2}{3} \div \frac{1}{4} =$

23/62

16) $\frac{1}{2} \div \frac{1}{2} =$

17) $\frac{1}{2} \div \frac{5}{6} =$

18) $\frac{1}{3} \div \frac{1}{7} =$

19) $\frac{2}{3} \div \frac{1}{2} =$

20) $\frac{1}{4} \div \frac{1}{3} =$

21) $\frac{2}{3} \div \frac{5}{7} =$

22) $\frac{2}{3} \div \frac{1}{3} =$

23) $1 \div \frac{1}{5} =$

24) $\frac{2}{5} \div \frac{1}{2} =$

25) $\frac{1}{4} \div \frac{3}{8} =$

26) $\frac{2}{3} \div \frac{3}{4} =$

27) $\frac{3}{5} \div \frac{3}{5} =$

28) $\frac{1}{3} \div \frac{1}{2} =$

29) $\frac{1}{2} \div \frac{5}{6} =$

30) $\frac{1}{2} \div \frac{1}{2} =$

1) $\frac{1}{2} \div \frac{2}{5} =$

2) $\frac{1}{4} \div \frac{3}{4} =$

3) $\frac{1}{3} \div \frac{2}{3} =$

4) $\frac{1}{2} \div \frac{5}{7} =$

5) $\frac{2}{3} \div \frac{5}{7} =$

6) $1 \div \frac{2}{3} =$

7) $\frac{1}{5} \div \frac{1}{6} =$

8) $\frac{1}{4} \div \frac{1}{2} =$

9) $\frac{1}{2} \div \frac{1}{2} =$

10) $\frac{2}{3} \div \frac{1}{4} =$

11) $\frac{2}{3} \div \frac{7}{8} =$

12) $\frac{1}{5} \div \frac{1}{5} =$

13) $\frac{1}{2} \div \frac{5}{6} =$

14) $\frac{3}{4} \div \frac{3}{4} =$

15) $\frac{3}{5} \div \frac{2}{5} =$

24/62

16) $\frac{1}{5} \div \frac{1}{3} =$

17) $\frac{1}{2} \div \frac{3}{7} =$

18) $\frac{3}{4} \div \frac{3}{4} =$

19) $\frac{1}{2} \div \frac{1}{2} =$

20) $\frac{2}{5} \div \frac{3}{4} =$

21) $\frac{1}{5} \div \frac{1}{2} =$

22) $\frac{4}{5} \div \frac{5}{7} =$

23) $\frac{3}{4} \div \frac{1}{7} =$

24) $\frac{3}{5} \div \frac{4}{5} =$

25) $\frac{1}{3} \div \frac{1}{2} =$

26) $\frac{1}{2} \div \frac{6}{7} =$

27) $\frac{1}{2} \div \frac{1}{7} =$

28) $\frac{3}{4} \div \frac{3}{8} =$

29) $\frac{1}{2} \div \frac{1}{7} =$

30) $\frac{3}{4} \div \frac{4}{7} =$

1) $\frac{1}{2} \div \frac{1}{2} =$ 2) $\frac{1}{2} \div \frac{7}{8} =$

3) $\frac{4}{5} \div \frac{2}{5} =$ 4) $\frac{1}{2} \div \frac{4}{5} =$

5) $\frac{3}{4} \div \frac{1}{2} =$ 6) $\frac{2}{3} \div \frac{5}{7} =$

7) $\frac{3}{5} \div \frac{2}{3} =$ 8) $\frac{1}{4} \div \frac{1}{2} =$

9) $\frac{1}{2} \div \frac{1}{3} =$ 10) $\frac{2}{3} \div \frac{1}{8} =$

11) $\frac{1}{2} \div \frac{1}{4} =$ 12) $\frac{1}{2} \div \frac{3}{4} =$

13) $\frac{1}{2} \div \frac{2}{3} =$ 14) $\frac{4}{5} \div \frac{1}{3} =$

15) $\frac{2}{5} \div \frac{1}{7} =$ 16) $\frac{3}{4} \div \frac{2}{7} =$

25/62

17) $\frac{1}{5} \div \frac{3}{4} =$ 18) $\frac{3}{4} \div \frac{1}{2} =$

19) $\frac{1}{2} \div \frac{2}{7} =$ 20) $\frac{4}{5} \div \frac{2}{3} =$

21) $\frac{1}{3} \div \frac{1}{2} =$ 22) $\frac{1}{3} \div \frac{3}{4} =$

23) $\frac{1}{5} \div \frac{1}{2} =$ 24) $\frac{1}{4} \div \frac{2}{3} =$

25) $\frac{1}{2} \div \frac{2}{5} =$ 26) $\frac{1}{3} \div \frac{5}{6} =$

27) $1 \div \frac{1}{7} =$ 28) $\frac{1}{2} \div \frac{1}{2} =$

29) $\frac{4}{5} \div \frac{2}{3} =$ 30) $\frac{3}{5} \div \frac{2}{5} =$

1) $\frac{1}{2} \div \frac{3}{4} =$

2) $\frac{3}{4} \div \frac{2}{3} =$

3) $\frac{1}{4} \div \frac{1}{2} =$

4) $\frac{1}{2} \div \frac{5}{6} =$

5) $\frac{3}{4} \div \frac{7}{8} =$

6) $\frac{1}{4} \div \frac{1}{3} =$

7) $\frac{1}{3} \div \frac{2}{5} =$

8) $\frac{2}{5} \div \frac{1}{2} =$

9) $\frac{1}{5} \div \frac{1}{2} =$

10) $\frac{1}{4} \div \frac{1}{2} =$

11) $\frac{4}{5} \div \frac{2}{3} =$

12) $\frac{1}{2} \div \frac{2}{3} =$

13) $\frac{1}{2} \div \frac{1}{6} =$

14) $\frac{1}{3} \div \frac{3}{7} =$

15) $\frac{1}{2} \div \frac{1}{3} =$

26/62

16) $\frac{2}{3} \div \frac{3}{4} =$

17) $\frac{3}{4} \div \frac{3}{4} =$

18) $\frac{2}{3} \div \frac{3}{7} =$

19) $\frac{1}{2} \div \frac{1}{2} =$

20) $\frac{1}{2} \div \frac{3}{7} =$

21) $\frac{1}{2} \div \frac{1}{4} =$

22) $\frac{2}{3} \div \frac{1}{2} =$

23) $\frac{1}{2} \div \frac{3}{8} =$

24) $\frac{1}{2} \div \frac{7}{8} =$

25) $\frac{1}{4} \div \frac{2}{5} =$

26) $\frac{2}{3} \div \frac{2}{3} =$

27) $\frac{4}{5} \div 1 =$

28) $\frac{1}{2} \div \frac{2}{5} =$

29) $\frac{2}{5} \div \frac{3}{8} =$

30) $\frac{3}{4} \div \frac{1}{3} =$

1) $\frac{1}{4} \div \frac{6}{7} =$

2) $\frac{1}{2} \div \frac{1}{2} =$

3) $\frac{1}{3} \div \frac{1}{4} =$

4) $\frac{3}{4} \div \frac{1}{5} =$

5) $\frac{4}{5} \div \frac{2}{3} =$

6) $\frac{1}{2} \div \frac{1}{3} =$

7) $\frac{2}{5} \div \frac{1}{8} =$

8) $\frac{1}{3} \div \frac{1}{3} =$

9) $\frac{2}{3} \div \frac{5}{6} =$

10) $\frac{3}{4} \div \frac{4}{5} =$

11) $\frac{1}{5} \div \frac{3}{8} =$

12) $\frac{2}{3} \div \frac{3}{7} =$

13) $\frac{4}{5} \div \frac{1}{2} =$

14) $\frac{2}{3} \div \frac{1}{2} =$

15) $\frac{1}{2} \div \frac{3}{4} =$

16) $\frac{1}{4} \div \frac{3}{4} =$

17) $\frac{1}{3} \div \frac{2}{5} =$

18) $\frac{2}{3} \div \frac{2}{7} =$

19) $\frac{1}{2} \div \frac{3}{4} =$

20) $\frac{1}{2} \div \frac{1}{2} =$

21) $\frac{2}{3} \div \frac{2}{3} =$

22) $\frac{1}{3} \div \frac{4}{7} =$

23) $\frac{1}{2} \div \frac{1}{8} =$

24) $\frac{2}{3} \div \frac{1}{3} =$

25) $\frac{1}{4} \div \frac{1}{4} =$

26) $\frac{1}{5} \div \frac{1}{4} =$

27) $\frac{1}{5} \div \frac{4}{7} =$

28) $1 \div \frac{3}{5} =$

29) $\frac{4}{5} \div \frac{1}{3} =$

30) $\frac{1}{2} \div \frac{1}{4} =$

27/62

1) $\frac{1}{2} \div \frac{3}{5} =$

2) $\frac{1}{2} \div 1 =$

3) $\frac{2}{5} \div \frac{2}{3} =$

4) $\frac{2}{3} \div \frac{1}{4} =$

5) $\frac{2}{3} \div \frac{4}{7} =$

6) $\frac{3}{4} \div \frac{1}{2} =$

7) $\frac{1}{2} \div \frac{1}{2} =$

8) $\frac{1}{5} \div \frac{1}{4} =$

9) $\frac{2}{3} \div \frac{3}{8} =$

10) $\frac{1}{2} \div \frac{7}{8} =$

11) $\frac{1}{4} \div \frac{3}{4} =$

12) $\frac{1}{2} \div \frac{1}{6} =$

13) $\frac{2}{5} \div \frac{4}{5} =$

14) $\frac{2}{3} \div \frac{2}{7} =$

15) $\frac{4}{5} \div \frac{4}{7} =$

16) $\frac{3}{4} \div \frac{6}{7} =$

28/62

17) $\frac{1}{2} \div \frac{1}{5} =$

18) $\frac{3}{5} \div \frac{3}{4} =$

19) $\frac{1}{3} \div \frac{1}{2} =$

20) $\frac{1}{5} \div \frac{4}{7} =$

21) $\frac{1}{3} \div \frac{4}{5} =$

22) $\frac{2}{3} \div \frac{1}{4} =$

23) $\frac{1}{2} \div \frac{1}{2} =$

24) $\frac{1}{2} \div \frac{2}{3} =$

25) $\frac{1}{2} \div \frac{1}{6} =$

26) $\frac{2}{5} \div \frac{1}{2} =$

27) $\frac{2}{3} \div \frac{5}{7} =$

28) $\frac{2}{3} \div \frac{1}{2} =$

29) $\frac{4}{5} \div \frac{1}{2} =$

30) $\frac{2}{3} \div \frac{3}{4} =$

1) $\frac{1}{2} \div \frac{1}{2} =$

2) $\frac{1}{3} \div \frac{1}{6} =$

3) $\frac{1}{2} \div \frac{1}{3} =$

4) $\frac{2}{3} \div \frac{2}{3} =$

5) $\frac{1}{3} \div \frac{1}{2} =$

6) $\frac{2}{5} \div \frac{1}{2} =$

7) $\frac{1}{3} \div \frac{1}{2} =$

8) $\frac{2}{3} \div \frac{1}{2} =$

9) $\frac{1}{2} \div \frac{1}{2} =$

10) $\frac{4}{5} \div \frac{3}{5} =$

11) $\frac{3}{5} \div \frac{5}{6} =$

12) $\frac{1}{2} \div \frac{1}{7} =$

13) $\frac{1}{3} \div \frac{3}{4} =$

14) $\frac{1}{2} \div \frac{3}{8} =$

15) $\frac{3}{5} \div \frac{3}{4} =$

16) $\frac{1}{3} \div \frac{2}{3} =$

17) $\frac{1}{5} \div \frac{2}{3} =$

18) $\frac{1}{4} \div \frac{1}{7} =$

19) $\frac{4}{5} \div \frac{1}{4} =$

20) $\frac{1}{2} \div \frac{4}{5} =$

21) $\frac{1}{2} \div \frac{1}{3} =$

22) $\frac{4}{5} \div \frac{1}{2} =$

23) $\frac{1}{2} \div \frac{4}{5} =$

24) $\frac{1}{2} \div \frac{1}{2} =$

25) $\frac{3}{5} \div \frac{2}{3} =$

26) $\frac{3}{4} \div \frac{2}{3} =$

27) $\frac{2}{5} \div \frac{3}{4} =$

28) $\frac{1}{2} \div \frac{3}{8} =$

29) $\frac{1}{2} \div \frac{2}{3} =$

30) $\frac{1}{4} \div \frac{1}{2} =$

1) $\frac{3}{5} \div \frac{2}{5} =$

2) $\frac{1}{3} \div \frac{3}{8} =$

3) $\frac{1}{3} \div \frac{7}{8} =$

4) $\frac{3}{5} \div \frac{1}{5} =$

5) $\frac{1}{2} \div \frac{1}{3} =$

6) $\frac{1}{2} \div \frac{2}{3} =$

7) $\frac{1}{5} \div \frac{2}{3} =$

8) $\frac{1}{2} \div \frac{1}{2} =$

9) $\frac{2}{5} \div \frac{5}{7} =$

10) $\frac{3}{4} \div \frac{1}{5} =$

11) $\frac{1}{4} \div \frac{1}{2} =$

12) $\frac{1}{2} \div \frac{1}{5} =$

13) $\frac{1}{2} \div \frac{3}{7} =$

14) $\frac{1}{3} \div \frac{1}{2} =$

15) $\frac{2}{3} \div \frac{1}{2} =$

30/62

16) $\frac{2}{3} \div \frac{2}{3} =$

17) $\frac{3}{4} \div \frac{2}{5} =$

18) $\frac{2}{5} \div \frac{1}{2} =$

19) $\frac{1}{2} \div \frac{2}{3} =$

20) $\frac{1}{2} \div \frac{1}{4} =$

21) $\frac{2}{5} \div \frac{5}{6} =$

22) $\frac{2}{5} \div \frac{1}{4} =$

23) $1 \div \frac{4}{5} =$

24) $\frac{1}{2} \div \frac{1}{4} =$

25) $\frac{3}{4} \div \frac{1}{2} =$

26) $\frac{1}{5} \div \frac{2}{3} =$

27) $\frac{3}{4} \div \frac{1}{4} =$

28) $\frac{1}{2} \div \frac{1}{2} =$

29) $\frac{1}{3} \div \frac{1}{3} =$

30) $\frac{2}{3} \div \frac{1}{3} =$

1) $5 \div \frac{13}{7} =$

2) $3 \div \frac{19}{6} =$

3) $\frac{15}{4} \div \frac{5}{3} =$

4) $4 \div \frac{7}{2} =$

5) $\frac{7}{2} \div \frac{5}{2} =$

6) $4 \div \frac{25}{6} =$

7) $\frac{8}{3} \div \frac{1}{4} =$

8) $1 \div \frac{23}{8} =$

9) $3 \div \frac{25}{7} =$

10) $\frac{6}{5} \div \frac{9}{2} =$

11) $\frac{1}{4} \div \frac{31}{7} =$

12) $\frac{9}{2} \div \frac{13}{7} =$

13) $\frac{9}{4} \div \frac{11}{2} =$

14) $\frac{12}{5} \div 5 =$

15) $\frac{2}{3} \div \frac{1}{2} =$

31/62

16) $1 \div \frac{4}{3} =$

17) $\frac{19}{4} \div \frac{17}{7} =$

18) $\frac{7}{4} \div \frac{29}{7} =$

19) $\frac{4}{5} \div \frac{25}{7} =$

20) $2 \div \frac{1}{5} =$

21) $\frac{3}{2} \div \frac{16}{5} =$

22) $\frac{8}{5} \div 5 =$

23) $\frac{13}{5} \div 3 =$

24) $1 \div \frac{5}{8} =$

25) $\frac{17}{4} \div \frac{25}{8} =$

26) $\frac{14}{5} \div \frac{2}{7} =$

27) $\frac{7}{3} \div \frac{19}{4} =$

28) $\frac{10}{3} \div \frac{1}{2} =$

29) $\frac{1}{3} \div \frac{10}{7} =$

30) $\frac{13}{5} \div \frac{29}{6} =$

1) $\frac{10}{3} \div \frac{15}{7} =$

2) $\frac{18}{5} \div \frac{1}{8} =$

3) $\frac{9}{2} \div \frac{1}{2} =$

4) $\frac{9}{4} \div \frac{13}{5} =$

5) $\frac{13}{4} \div \frac{17}{6} =$

6) $4 \div \frac{15}{4} =$

7) $\frac{7}{2} \div \frac{19}{7} =$

8) $\frac{7}{3} \div 2 =$

9) $3 \div \frac{18}{5} =$

10) $\frac{5}{2} \div \frac{2}{7} =$

11) $\frac{1}{3} \div \frac{7}{2} =$

12) $2 \div \frac{10}{7} =$

13) $\frac{1}{5} \div 2 =$

14) $\frac{4}{3} \div \frac{17}{4} =$

15) $\frac{7}{3} \div \frac{2}{5} =$

16) $\frac{3}{2} \div 5 =$

17) $\frac{21}{5} \div 3 =$

18) $\frac{9}{2} \div \frac{21}{4} =$

19) $\frac{1}{3} \div \frac{3}{4} =$

20) $4 \div \frac{11}{3} =$

21) $\frac{13}{4} \div \frac{13}{3} =$

22) $\frac{8}{3} \div \frac{13}{4} =$

23) $\frac{14}{3} \div \frac{9}{5} =$

24) $3 \div \frac{5}{2} =$

25) $\frac{17}{5} \div \frac{15}{8} =$

26) $\frac{14}{5} \div \frac{6}{5} =$

27) $\frac{8}{5} \div \frac{5}{2} =$

28) $\frac{21}{4} \div \frac{25}{8} =$

29) $\frac{3}{2} \div 1 =$

30) $2 \div \frac{2}{5} =$

1) $\frac{5}{4} \div \frac{3}{2} =$

2) $\frac{1}{2} \div \frac{13}{3} =$

3) $5 \div \frac{17}{6} =$

4) $\frac{3}{2} \div \frac{22}{7} =$

5) $\frac{3}{2} \div \frac{24}{7} =$

6) $2 \div \frac{17}{6} =$

7) $\frac{2}{3} \div \frac{11}{3} =$

8) $\frac{7}{2} \div \frac{13}{5} =$

9) $\frac{5}{2} \div 2 =$

10) $4 \div \frac{8}{3} =$

11) $\frac{13}{4} \div \frac{29}{6} =$

12) $\frac{1}{5} \div \frac{5}{8} =$

13) $5 \div \frac{4}{5} =$

14) $4 \div \frac{10}{7} =$

15) $\frac{1}{2} \div \frac{17}{5} =$

33/62

16) $\frac{17}{5} \div 1 =$

17) $\frac{13}{4} \div \frac{9}{2} =$

18) $\frac{13}{3} \div \frac{17}{7} =$

19) $\frac{13}{4} \div \frac{5}{3} =$

20) $\frac{2}{5} \div \frac{29}{7} =$

21) $\frac{3}{2} \div \frac{35}{8} =$

22) $1 \div \frac{25}{8} =$

23) $2 \div \frac{11}{3} =$

24) $5 \div \frac{4}{3} =$

25) $\frac{1}{4} \div \frac{11}{5} =$

26) $2 \div \frac{3}{5} =$

27) $\frac{9}{2} \div 1 =$

28) $5 \div \frac{16}{5} =$

29) $\frac{5}{3} \div 5 =$

30) $\frac{1}{3} \div \frac{3}{4} =$

1) $\frac{16}{5} \div \frac{11}{3} =$

2) $\frac{7}{3} \div \frac{19}{5} =$

3) $\frac{1}{4} \div \frac{3}{2} =$

4) $1 \div \frac{19}{4} =$

5) $\frac{13}{4} \div \frac{17}{4} =$

6) $\frac{10}{3} \div \frac{2}{3} =$

7) $\frac{11}{3} \div \frac{19}{4} =$

8) $1 \div \frac{9}{5} =$

9) $\frac{3}{5} \div \frac{1}{2} =$

10) $\frac{3}{4} \div \frac{13}{3} =$

11) $\frac{13}{5} \div \frac{16}{7} =$

12) $\frac{24}{5} \div \frac{10}{3} =$

13) $2 \div \frac{5}{3} =$

14) $5 \div \frac{23}{8} =$

15) $\frac{5}{2} \div 1 =$

34/62

16) $\frac{17}{4} \div \frac{9}{4} =$

17) $3 \div \frac{19}{6} =$

18) $4 \div \frac{7}{5} =$

19) $3 \div \frac{6}{7} =$

20) $\frac{10}{3} \div \frac{9}{8} =$

21) $\frac{4}{3} \div \frac{4}{7} =$

22) $\frac{1}{3} \div \frac{1}{3} =$

23) $\frac{1}{2} \div 3 =$

24) $\frac{2}{5} \div \frac{29}{6} =$

25) $4 \div \frac{13}{4} =$

26) $\frac{2}{3} \div 5 =$

27) $\frac{19}{5} \div 4 =$

28) $\frac{1}{2} \div 1 =$

29) $\frac{1}{3} \div 4 =$

30) $\frac{18}{5} \div \frac{32}{7} =$

1) $\frac{7}{2} \div \frac{14}{3} =$

2) $\frac{18}{5} \div 2 =$

3) $\frac{22}{5} \div \frac{7}{2} =$

4) $\frac{21}{5} \div \frac{5}{2} =$

5) $\frac{1}{2} \div \frac{11}{5} =$

6) $5 \div \frac{33}{8} =$

7) $1 \div \frac{11}{5} =$

8) $\frac{2}{3} \div \frac{7}{3} =$

9) $\frac{7}{2} \div 2 =$

10) $2 \div \frac{25}{6} =$

11) $3 \div \frac{4}{3} =$

12) $1 \div \frac{5}{4} =$

13) $\frac{11}{5} \div 3 =$

14) $\frac{1}{4} \div \frac{15}{4} =$

15) $\frac{24}{5} \div \frac{16}{5} =$

35/62

16) $\frac{10}{3} \div \frac{31}{8} =$

17) $\frac{11}{2} \div \frac{7}{2} =$

18) $\frac{1}{4} \div \frac{7}{3} =$

19) $5 \div \frac{2}{7} =$

20) $\frac{8}{3} \div \frac{5}{7} =$

21) $\frac{9}{2} \div 2 =$

22) $\frac{2}{3} \div \frac{12}{7} =$

23) $4 \div \frac{1}{2} =$

24) $4 \div \frac{16}{7} =$

25) $\frac{21}{5} \div \frac{27}{8} =$

26) $\frac{5}{3} \div \frac{15}{4} =$

27) $2 \div \frac{5}{2} =$

28) $\frac{3}{4} \div 5 =$

29) $\frac{7}{2} \div \frac{32}{7} =$

30) $\frac{5}{2} \div \frac{3}{7} =$

1) $\frac{2}{5} \div \frac{33}{7} =$

2) $\frac{7}{3} \div \frac{7}{3} =$

3) $\frac{4}{5} \div 1 =$

4) $2 \div \frac{1}{5} =$

5) $\frac{7}{4} \div 1 =$

6) $\frac{5}{2} \div \frac{2}{3} =$

7) $1 \div \frac{7}{6} =$

8) $\frac{1}{3} \div \frac{18}{5} =$

9) $1 \div \frac{17}{7} =$

10) $\frac{6}{5} \div \frac{16}{5} =$

11) $\frac{17}{5} \div \frac{13}{4} =$

12) $\frac{14}{5} \div 4 =$

13) $\frac{11}{2} \div \frac{17}{4} =$

14) $\frac{8}{5} \div \frac{22}{5} =$

15) $\frac{7}{2} \div \frac{7}{2} =$

36/62

16) $\frac{2}{3} \div 2 =$

17) $5 \div \frac{13}{6} =$

18) $\frac{15}{4} \div 2 =$

19) $3 \div \frac{1}{5} =$

20) $4 \div \frac{24}{5} =$

21) $\frac{8}{5} \div 2 =$

22) $\frac{7}{2} \div \frac{7}{4} =$

23) $2 \div \frac{22}{7} =$

24) $\frac{3}{5} \div \frac{3}{4} =$

25) $\frac{2}{3} \div \frac{5}{4} =$

26) $\frac{9}{2} \div \frac{3}{4} =$

27) $1 \div \frac{7}{2} =$

28) $\frac{1}{2} \div 5 =$

29) $\frac{10}{3} \div \frac{1}{8} =$

30) $2 \div \frac{8}{3} =$

1) $\frac{1}{3} \div 3 =$

2) $\frac{15}{4} \div 2 =$

3) $1 \div \frac{5}{3} =$

4) $\frac{13}{3} \div \frac{7}{3} =$

5) $\frac{4}{3} \div \frac{6}{5} =$

6) $2 \div \frac{17}{7} =$

7) $1 \div \frac{2}{5} =$

8) $\frac{7}{3} \div 4 =$

9) $\frac{7}{2} \div \frac{3}{2} =$

10) $\frac{4}{3} \div \frac{4}{3} =$

11) $1 \div \frac{20}{7} =$

12) $\frac{7}{3} \div \frac{11}{4} =$

13) $\frac{3}{2} \div \frac{8}{7} =$

14) $\frac{4}{5} \div \frac{3}{2} =$

15) $4 \div \frac{3}{2} =$

37/62

16) $\frac{23}{5} \div 1 =$

17) $\frac{7}{3} \div \frac{4}{3} =$

18) $4 \div \frac{1}{3} =$

19) $1 \div \frac{8}{5} =$

20) $\frac{19}{4} \div 5 =$

21) $\frac{23}{5} \div \frac{7}{2} =$

22) $5 \div \frac{13}{3} =$

23) $\frac{3}{2} \div \frac{8}{3} =$

24) $\frac{10}{3} \div \frac{33}{7} =$

25) $\frac{7}{3} \div \frac{9}{4} =$

26) $2 \div \frac{12}{5} =$

27) $2 \div \frac{22}{5} =$

28) $3 \div \frac{7}{4} =$

29) $\frac{1}{2} \div \frac{3}{2} =$

30) $\frac{24}{5} \div \frac{19}{4} =$

1) $\frac{1}{2} \div \frac{4}{7} =$

2) $\frac{4}{5} \div \frac{1}{8} =$

3) $\frac{1}{6} \div \frac{2}{3} =$

4) $\frac{1}{5} \div \frac{6}{7} =$

5) $\frac{3}{4} \div \frac{4}{5} =$

6) $\frac{3}{5} \div \frac{3}{10} =$

7) $\frac{2}{5} \div \frac{5}{6} =$

8) $\frac{2}{3} \div \frac{1}{2} =$

9) $\frac{3}{7} \div \frac{1}{2} =$

10) $\frac{3}{4} \div \frac{1}{2} =$

11) $\frac{1}{5} \div \frac{1}{3} =$

12) $\frac{1}{2} \div \frac{1}{2} =$

13) $\frac{1}{3} \div \frac{4}{5} =$

14) $\frac{5}{6} \div \frac{2}{3} =$

15) $\frac{1}{3} \div \frac{6}{7} =$

16) $\frac{5}{6} \div \frac{1}{2} =$

17) $\frac{1}{8} \div \frac{2}{3} =$

18) $\frac{8}{9} \div \frac{8}{9} =$

19) $\frac{5}{6} \div \frac{1}{2} =$

20) $\frac{4}{5} \div \frac{3}{4} =$

21) $\frac{1}{2} \div \frac{1}{3} =$

22) $\frac{1}{4} \div \frac{6}{7} =$

23) $\frac{4}{5} \div \frac{1}{2} =$

24) $\frac{2}{3} \div \frac{5}{7} =$

25) $\frac{2}{3} \div \frac{2}{5} =$

26) $\frac{4}{5} \div \frac{1}{4} =$

27) $\frac{1}{5} \div \frac{5}{7} =$

28) $\frac{3}{5} \div \frac{1}{3} =$

29) $\frac{1}{2} \div \frac{1}{4} =$

30) $\frac{4}{5} \div \frac{3}{4} =$

38/62

1) $\frac{7}{9} \div \frac{5}{7} =$

2) $\frac{7}{10} \div \frac{1}{2} =$

3) $\frac{1}{8} \div \frac{5}{6} =$

4) $\frac{1}{3} \div \frac{3}{8} =$

5) $\frac{1}{3} \div \frac{1}{2} =$

6) $\frac{1}{6} \div \frac{1}{2} =$

7) $\frac{7}{8} \div 1 =$

8) $\frac{7}{8} \div \frac{2}{5} =$

9) $\frac{1}{3} \div \frac{3}{5} =$

10) $\frac{2}{9} \div \frac{1}{2} =$

11) $\frac{1}{2} \div \frac{1}{5} =$

12) $\frac{3}{10} \div \frac{5}{7} =$

13) $\frac{2}{3} \div \frac{3}{4} =$

14) $\frac{1}{2} \div \frac{1}{7} =$

15) $\frac{1}{3} \div \frac{1}{7} =$

39/62

16) $\frac{1}{2} \div \frac{1}{4} =$

17) $\frac{5}{6} \div \frac{7}{9} =$

18) $\frac{1}{2} \div \frac{2}{3} =$

19) $\frac{1}{2} \div \frac{3}{8} =$

20) $\frac{2}{5} \div \frac{5}{6} =$

21) $\frac{1}{4} \div \frac{4}{5} =$

22) $\frac{1}{2} \div \frac{2}{3} =$

23) $\frac{2}{5} \div \frac{1}{2} =$

24) $\frac{1}{2} \div \frac{3}{5} =$

25) $\frac{1}{5} \div \frac{1}{2} =$

26) $\frac{3}{5} \div \frac{1}{2} =$

27) $\frac{6}{7} \div \frac{2}{5} =$

28) $\frac{3}{10} \div \frac{5}{9} =$

29) $\frac{1}{2} \div \frac{3}{5} =$

30) $\frac{6}{7} \div \frac{1}{3} =$

1) $\frac{1}{2} \div \frac{2}{5} =$

2) $\frac{1}{3} \div \frac{1}{3} =$

3) $\frac{9}{10} \div \frac{1}{3} =$

4) $\frac{6}{7} \div \frac{5}{6} =$

5) $\frac{1}{2} \div \frac{3}{10} =$

6) $\frac{3}{4} \div \frac{1}{4} =$

7) $\frac{3}{8} \div \frac{5}{6} =$

8) $\frac{4}{9} \div \frac{1}{5} =$

9) $\frac{3}{10} \div \frac{2}{3} =$

10) $\frac{1}{3} \div \frac{4}{5} =$

11) $\frac{1}{10} \div \frac{1}{3} =$

12) $\frac{5}{7} \div \frac{1}{2} =$

13) $\frac{1}{2} \div \frac{1}{2} =$

14) $\frac{2}{7} \div \frac{6}{7} =$

15) $\frac{1}{2} \div \frac{1}{3} =$

40/62

16) $\frac{3}{5} \div \frac{1}{2} =$

17) $\frac{1}{2} \div \frac{1}{3} =$

18) $\frac{5}{8} \div \frac{1}{2} =$

19) $\frac{2}{3} \div \frac{5}{6} =$

20) $\frac{1}{4} \div \frac{3}{7} =$

21) $\frac{4}{5} \div \frac{1}{9} =$

22) $\frac{4}{7} \div \frac{4}{5} =$

23) $\frac{2}{3} \div \frac{2}{5} =$

24) $\frac{3}{7} \div \frac{5}{6} =$

25) $\frac{4}{5} \div \frac{2}{3} =$

26) $\frac{2}{3} \div \frac{1}{7} =$

27) $\frac{1}{3} \div 1 =$

28) $\frac{1}{2} \div \frac{2}{3} =$

29) $\frac{4}{5} \div \frac{3}{4} =$

30) $\frac{2}{5} \div \frac{4}{5} =$

Multiplying and Dividing Fractions

1) $\frac{6}{7} \div \frac{3}{8} =$

2) $\frac{7}{8} \times \frac{1}{2} =$

3) $\frac{2}{5} \div \frac{1}{6} =$

4) $\frac{5}{6} \times \frac{1}{6} =$

5) $\frac{3}{5} \times \frac{5}{6} =$

6) $\frac{2}{5} \div \frac{1}{6} =$

7) $\frac{3}{4} \div \frac{1}{4} =$

8) $\frac{1}{3} \times \frac{2}{5} =$

9) $\frac{3}{5} \times \frac{4}{5} =$

10) $\frac{5}{6} \div \frac{4}{5} =$

11) $\frac{7}{9} \times \frac{2}{7} =$

12) $\frac{1}{5} \div \frac{8}{9} =$

13) $\frac{7}{8} \div \frac{2}{5} =$

41/62

14) $\frac{5}{9} \div \frac{1}{3} =$

15) $\frac{5}{6} \times \frac{1}{3} =$

16) $\frac{2}{9} \times \frac{1}{3} =$

17) $\frac{2}{3} \times \frac{2}{7} =$

18) $\frac{2}{9} \times \frac{1}{2} =$

19) $\frac{5}{9} \div \frac{3}{4} =$

20) $\frac{1}{2} \div \frac{4}{5} =$

21) $\frac{1}{2} \times \frac{1}{6} =$

22) $\frac{3}{4} \div \frac{4}{7} =$

23) $\frac{1}{8} \div \frac{1}{2} =$

24) $\frac{2}{3} \times \frac{5}{8} =$

25) $\frac{6}{7} \times \frac{7}{9} =$

26) $\frac{7}{9} \times \frac{2}{7} =$

27) $\frac{1}{4} \div \frac{1}{4} =$

28) $\frac{4}{7} \div \frac{1}{9} =$

29) $\frac{1}{3} \times \frac{1}{5} =$

30) $\frac{3}{4} \div \frac{8}{9} =$

1) $\frac{2}{3} \times \frac{3}{8} =$

2) $\frac{7}{10} \times \frac{2}{3} =$

3) $\frac{3}{4} \div \frac{1}{2} =$

4) $\frac{1}{3} \div \frac{1}{3} =$

5) $\frac{1}{6} \times \frac{1}{2} =$

6) $\frac{3}{4} \times \frac{1}{2} =$

7) $\frac{1}{9} \div \frac{2}{3} =$

8) $\frac{5}{7} \div \frac{2}{3} =$

9) $\frac{8}{9} \times \frac{2}{3} =$

10) $\frac{8}{9} \times \frac{5}{7} =$

11) $\frac{3}{4} \div \frac{1}{2} =$

12) $\frac{2}{3} \div \frac{1}{5} =$

13) $\frac{1}{5} \times \frac{2}{3} =$

14) $\frac{1}{2} \times \frac{2}{3} =$

15) $\frac{4}{7} \div \frac{8}{9} =$

42/62

16) $\frac{1}{4} \div \frac{3}{4} =$

17) $\frac{1}{5} \div \frac{1}{4} =$

18) $\frac{1}{7} \times \frac{2}{3} =$

19) $1 \div \frac{1}{2} =$

20) $\frac{1}{6} \times \frac{4}{5} =$

21) $\frac{1}{7} \div \frac{3}{8} =$

22) $\frac{3}{4} \div \frac{2}{3} =$

23) $\frac{3}{4} \times \frac{9}{10} =$

24) $\frac{1}{9} \times \frac{1}{2} =$

25) $\frac{4}{5} \div \frac{3}{5} =$

26) $\frac{2}{3} \times \frac{1}{2} =$

27) $\frac{7}{8} \div \frac{1}{10} =$

28) $\frac{4}{7} \times \frac{1}{2} =$

29) $\frac{6}{7} \times \frac{2}{3} =$

30) $\frac{1}{8} \times \frac{5}{6} =$

1) $\frac{6}{7} \div \frac{1}{4} =$

2) $\frac{1}{7} \times \frac{1}{2} =$

3) $\frac{5}{7} \times \frac{1}{2} =$

4) $\frac{1}{4} \div \frac{2}{3} =$

5) $\frac{5}{6} \div \frac{7}{8} =$

6) $\frac{2}{7} \times \frac{1}{3} =$

7) $\frac{5}{7} \times \frac{2}{5} =$

8) $\frac{7}{8} \div \frac{2}{5} =$

9) $\frac{1}{2} \div \frac{2}{3} =$

10) $\frac{3}{4} \times \frac{1}{2} =$

11) $\frac{5}{6} \div \frac{1}{2} =$

12) $\frac{1}{4} \times \frac{2}{3} =$

13) $\frac{1}{2} \times \frac{7}{10} =$

14) $\frac{2}{5} \div \frac{7}{10} =$

15) $\frac{4}{9} \div \frac{3}{5} =$

16) $\frac{6}{7} \times \frac{1}{2} =$

17) $\frac{4}{5} \div \frac{4}{5} =$

18) $\frac{1}{2} \times \frac{1}{2} =$

19) $\frac{1}{3} \div \frac{1}{3} =$

20) $\frac{4}{9} \times \frac{4}{5} =$

21) $\frac{1}{6} \times \frac{3}{5} =$

22) $\frac{3}{4} \times \frac{2}{3} =$

23) $\frac{4}{9} \div \frac{1}{2} =$

24) $\frac{1}{2} \div \frac{2}{5} =$

25) $\frac{7}{9} \div \frac{1}{4} =$

26) $\frac{3}{4} \times \frac{1}{2} =$

27) $\frac{7}{10} \times \frac{1}{2} =$

28) $\frac{1}{9} \div \frac{3}{7} =$

29) $\frac{3}{4} \div \frac{1}{3} =$

30) $\frac{7}{8} \times \frac{1}{4} =$

43/62

1) $\frac{1}{4} \times \frac{4}{5} =$

2) $\frac{1}{2} \div \frac{1}{2} =$

3) $\frac{1}{5} \div \frac{1}{2} =$

4) $1 \times \frac{1}{3} =$

5) $\frac{1}{2} \div \frac{1}{2} =$

6) $\frac{1}{3} \div \frac{1}{5} =$

7) $\frac{2}{9} \times \frac{1}{4} =$

8) $\frac{4}{7} \times \frac{3}{8} =$

9) $\frac{3}{4} \times \frac{1}{2} =$

10) $\frac{2}{7} \times \frac{5}{8} =$

11) $\frac{2}{5} \div \frac{1}{3} =$

12) $\frac{1}{2} \div \frac{5}{7} =$

13) $\frac{1}{2} \div \frac{4}{5} =$

14) $\frac{7}{10} \times \frac{7}{8} =$

15) $\frac{1}{5} \times \frac{2}{3} =$

44/62

16) $\frac{3}{4} \div \frac{1}{4} =$

17) $\frac{9}{10} \div \frac{1}{3} =$

18) $\frac{7}{10} \div \frac{1}{2} =$

19) $\frac{2}{3} \times \frac{1}{4} =$

20) $\frac{2}{5} \times \frac{1}{2} =$

21) $\frac{2}{3} \div \frac{2}{3} =$

22) $\frac{1}{2} \div \frac{1}{7} =$

23) $\frac{2}{3} \times \frac{2}{3} =$

24) $\frac{1}{2} \times \frac{3}{4} =$

25) $\frac{1}{3} \times \frac{1}{3} =$

26) $\frac{1}{5} \div \frac{4}{5} =$

27) $\frac{7}{9} \div \frac{3}{5} =$

28) $\frac{2}{3} \times \frac{1}{2} =$

29) $\frac{3}{4} \div \frac{1}{6} =$

30) $\frac{1}{2} \times \frac{4}{5} =$

1) $\frac{1}{8} \div \frac{1}{2} =$

2) $\frac{1}{2} \times \frac{1}{3} =$

3) $\frac{1}{3} \times \frac{2}{7} =$

4) $\frac{3}{10} \div \frac{2}{5} =$

5) $\frac{4}{5} \times \frac{3}{4} =$

6) $\frac{1}{2} \div \frac{1}{5} =$

7) $\frac{1}{6} \div \frac{2}{5} =$

8) $\frac{5}{6} \times \frac{1}{2} =$

9) $\frac{5}{8} \div \frac{1}{2} =$

10) $\frac{1}{2} \div \frac{3}{7} =$

11) $\frac{3}{4} \times \frac{1}{5} =$

12) $\frac{1}{2} \times \frac{1}{3} =$

13) $\frac{2}{3} \div \frac{1}{4} =$

14) $\frac{5}{6} \times \frac{1}{2} =$

15) $\frac{1}{2} \times \frac{3}{5} =$

45/62

16) $\frac{1}{2} \div \frac{1}{5} =$

17) $\frac{1}{2} \times \frac{2}{5} =$

18) $\frac{4}{7} \times 1 =$

19) $\frac{3}{8} \div \frac{2}{5} =$

20) $\frac{1}{3} \div \frac{4}{9} =$

21) $\frac{1}{2} \div \frac{1}{6} =$

22) $\frac{1}{6} \times \frac{2}{3} =$

23) $\frac{1}{2} \div \frac{3}{7} =$

24) $\frac{1}{2} \times \frac{1}{3} =$

25) $\frac{4}{5} \times \frac{1}{2} =$

26) $\frac{1}{2} \div \frac{1}{2} =$

27) $\frac{4}{7} \div \frac{3}{4} =$

28) $\frac{4}{7} \times \frac{1}{4} =$

29) $\frac{3}{4} \times \frac{3}{5} =$

30) $\frac{2}{5} \times \frac{1}{2} =$

1) $\frac{1}{5} \times \frac{1}{2} =$

2) $\frac{1}{2} \div \frac{1}{3} =$

3) $\frac{7}{8} \div \frac{1}{2} =$

4) $\frac{3}{4} \times \frac{5}{8} =$

5) $\frac{3}{4} \times 1 =$

6) $\frac{1}{4} \times \frac{2}{5} =$

7) $\frac{1}{2} \div \frac{5}{7} =$

8) $\frac{8}{9} \div \frac{3}{8} =$

9) $\frac{1}{2} \times \frac{3}{4} =$

10) $\frac{5}{9} \times \frac{2}{3} =$

11) $\frac{1}{2} \div \frac{2}{5} =$

12) $\frac{3}{4} \div \frac{1}{2} =$

13) $\frac{3}{5} \div \frac{1}{2} =$

14) $\frac{7}{10} \times \frac{5}{8} =$

15) $\frac{1}{4} \times \frac{3}{5} =$

46/62

16) $\frac{1}{3} \div \frac{1}{2} =$

17) $\frac{4}{7} \div \frac{2}{5} =$

18) $\frac{1}{5} \times \frac{1}{3} =$

19) $\frac{4}{5} \times \frac{2}{5} =$

20) $\frac{4}{5} \div \frac{3}{8} =$

21) $\frac{1}{4} \div \frac{1}{3} =$

22) $\frac{4}{9} \times \frac{6}{7} =$

23) $\frac{1}{3} \div \frac{5}{7} =$

24) $\frac{3}{5} \times \frac{1}{2} =$

25) $\frac{1}{5} \div \frac{7}{9} =$

26) $\frac{2}{3} \times \frac{2}{3} =$

27) $\frac{1}{2} \times \frac{4}{9} =$

28) $\frac{1}{4} \div \frac{1}{4} =$

29) $\frac{5}{8} \div \frac{1}{2} =$

30) $\frac{1}{2} \div \frac{1}{3} =$

1) $\frac{7}{9} \div \frac{2}{3} =$

2) $\frac{2}{3} \times \frac{6}{7} =$

3) $\frac{7}{8} \div \frac{4}{7} =$

4) $\frac{1}{9} \times \frac{2}{3} =$

5) $\frac{1}{2} \div \frac{5}{6} =$

6) $\frac{1}{8} \times \frac{1}{2} =$

7) $\frac{1}{2} \div \frac{1}{4} =$

8) $\frac{6}{7} \times \frac{2}{5} =$

9) $\frac{1}{2} \div \frac{1}{9} =$

10) $\frac{3}{4} \times \frac{4}{9} =$

11) $\frac{1}{4} \times \frac{3}{5} =$

12) $\frac{1}{2} \div \frac{1}{2} =$

13) $\frac{1}{2} \times \frac{2}{3} =$

14) $\frac{1}{4} \div \frac{2}{3} =$

15) $\frac{1}{5} \div \frac{1}{5} =$

47/62

16) $\frac{2}{3} \times \frac{1}{3} =$

17) $\frac{4}{5} \times \frac{1}{3} =$

18) $\frac{4}{5} \div \frac{5}{6} =$

19) $\frac{4}{5} \div \frac{1}{2} =$

20) $\frac{6}{7} \times \frac{1}{3} =$

21) $1 \times \frac{7}{10} =$

22) $\frac{2}{3} \times \frac{1}{3} =$

23) $\frac{1}{9} \div \frac{2}{3} =$

24) $\frac{1}{2} \div \frac{1}{2} =$

25) $\frac{9}{10} \times \frac{1}{2} =$

26) $\frac{4}{5} \div \frac{1}{2} =$

27) $\frac{2}{5} \div \frac{1}{5} =$

28) $\frac{1}{5} \times \frac{1}{2} =$

29) $\frac{2}{3} \times \frac{1}{4} =$

30) $\frac{4}{7} \div \frac{3}{7} =$

1) $\frac{3}{5} \times \frac{1}{10} =$

2) $\frac{2}{3} \times \frac{3}{10} =$

3) $\frac{1}{5} \div \frac{1}{2} =$

4) $\frac{1}{3} \div \frac{1}{2} =$

5) $\frac{1}{4} \div \frac{5}{6} =$

6) $\frac{3}{5} \div \frac{2}{5} =$

7) $\frac{1}{2} \times \frac{2}{3} =$

8) $\frac{1}{3} \times \frac{1}{6} =$

9) $\frac{1}{6} \div \frac{3}{5} =$

10) $\frac{1}{5} \div 1 =$

11) $\frac{1}{2} \times \frac{2}{3} =$

12) $\frac{4}{5} \times \frac{1}{3} =$

13) $\frac{2}{3} \div \frac{1}{2} =$

14) $\frac{2}{3} \times \frac{4}{5} =$

15) $\frac{1}{2} \div \frac{1}{7} =$

48/62

16) $\frac{2}{3} \times \frac{1}{2} =$

17) $\frac{2}{3} \times \frac{3}{4} =$

18) $\frac{1}{3} \div \frac{1}{2} =$

19) $\frac{4}{9} \div \frac{5}{9} =$

20) $\frac{1}{2} \times \frac{1}{5} =$

21) $\frac{2}{3} \div \frac{1}{2} =$

22) $\frac{4}{5} \times \frac{4}{9} =$

23) $\frac{3}{4} \times \frac{1}{2} =$

24) $\frac{1}{10} \div \frac{2}{5} =$

25) $\frac{3}{8} \div \frac{1}{5} =$

26) $\frac{1}{2} \times \frac{8}{9} =$

27) $\frac{1}{3} \div \frac{5}{6} =$

28) $\frac{3}{4} \times \frac{1}{4} =$

29) $\frac{1}{4} \div \frac{1}{4} =$

30) $\frac{1}{2} \times \frac{3}{4} =$

1) $\frac{3}{4} \times \frac{1}{2} =$

2) $\frac{2}{3} \div \frac{1}{5} =$

3) $\frac{8}{9} \times \frac{1}{2} =$

4) $\frac{3}{5} \div \frac{2}{3} =$

5) $\frac{4}{5} \times \frac{2}{5} =$

6) $\frac{7}{9} \times \frac{1}{7} =$

7) $\frac{1}{3} \div 1 =$

8) $\frac{2}{3} \div \frac{3}{5} =$

9) $\frac{1}{7} \div \frac{5}{8} =$

10) $\frac{2}{7} \div \frac{5}{7} =$

11) $\frac{3}{5} \times \frac{1}{7} =$

12) $\frac{1}{2} \times \frac{3}{5} =$

13) $\frac{1}{6} \times \frac{1}{3} =$

14) $\frac{4}{9} \times \frac{1}{7} =$

15) $\frac{2}{3} \div \frac{1}{2} =$

49/62

16) $\frac{3}{4} \div \frac{1}{3} =$

17) $\frac{7}{8} \times \frac{2}{5} =$

18) $\frac{6}{7} \div \frac{1}{2} =$

19) $\frac{7}{8} \div \frac{2}{5} =$

20) $\frac{3}{5} \times \frac{1}{4} =$

21) $\frac{9}{10} \times \frac{2}{3} =$

22) $\frac{1}{6} \times \frac{1}{2} =$

23) $\frac{3}{4} \div \frac{2}{3} =$

24) $\frac{9}{10} \div \frac{3}{5} =$

25) $\frac{2}{3} \div \frac{1}{9} =$

26) $\frac{1}{2} \times \frac{4}{5} =$

27) $\frac{4}{5} \div \frac{1}{5} =$

28) $\frac{1}{2} \times \frac{1}{10} =$

29) $\frac{4}{5} \div \frac{1}{2} =$

30) $\frac{2}{5} \times \frac{3}{5} =$

1) $\frac{5}{7} \div \frac{1}{4} =$

2) $\frac{2}{3} \times \frac{7}{10} =$

3) $\frac{3}{4} \div \frac{1}{7} =$

4) $\frac{3}{4} \times \frac{2}{5} =$

5) $1 \div \frac{8}{9} =$

6) $\frac{1}{2} \times \frac{3}{4} =$

7) $\frac{5}{7} \div \frac{2}{3} =$

8) $\frac{2}{5} \times \frac{2}{3} =$

9) $\frac{3}{4} \times \frac{3}{5} =$

10) $\frac{5}{7} \div \frac{2}{7} =$

11) $\frac{7}{10} \times \frac{2}{9} =$

12) $\frac{1}{9} \div \frac{2}{3} =$

13) $\frac{2}{5} \times \frac{1}{2} =$

14) $1 \div \frac{1}{2} =$

15) $\frac{1}{2} \div \frac{2}{5} =$

50/62

16) $\frac{8}{9} \times \frac{4}{5} =$

17) $\frac{2}{7} \times \frac{1}{8} =$

18) $\frac{2}{5} \div \frac{4}{7} =$

19) $\frac{1}{2} \div \frac{1}{3} =$

20) $\frac{4}{5} \times \frac{1}{2} =$

21) $\frac{2}{3} \times \frac{1}{2} =$

22) $\frac{2}{7} \times \frac{1}{4} =$

23) $\frac{1}{2} \div \frac{3}{5} =$

24) $\frac{1}{8} \div \frac{1}{2} =$

25) $\frac{1}{2} \div \frac{1}{4} =$

26) $\frac{9}{10} \times \frac{1}{4} =$

27) $\frac{7}{8} \times \frac{1}{5} =$

28) $\frac{2}{3} \div \frac{3}{10} =$

29) $\frac{1}{6} \times \frac{5}{7} =$

30) $\frac{1}{4} \div \frac{1}{2} =$

1) $\frac{5}{9} \times \frac{3}{5} =$ 2) $\frac{2}{3} \times \frac{8}{9} =$

3) $\frac{1}{3} \div \frac{9}{10} =$ 4) $\frac{1}{9} \div \frac{2}{7} =$

5) $\frac{3}{8} \div \frac{5}{7} =$ 6) $\frac{1}{10} \times \frac{2}{3} =$

7) $\frac{4}{5} \times \frac{1}{2} =$ 8) $\frac{1}{2} \div \frac{1}{2} =$

9) $\frac{2}{3} \times \frac{4}{7} =$ 10) $\frac{1}{2} \div \frac{4}{9} =$

11) $\frac{2}{3} \div \frac{1}{2} =$ 12) $\frac{1}{10} \times \frac{1}{5} =$

13) $\frac{4}{7} \times \frac{1}{3} =$ 14) $\frac{3}{7} \div \frac{3}{10} =$

15) $\frac{7}{8} \div \frac{1}{2} =$ **51/62**   16) $\frac{3}{4} \times \frac{1}{2} =$

17) $\frac{5}{7} \div \frac{1}{5} =$ 18) $\frac{3}{8} \times \frac{1}{3} =$

19) $\frac{1}{5} \div \frac{7}{8} =$ 20) $\frac{1}{2} \times \frac{1}{2} =$

21) $\frac{1}{8} \div \frac{1}{9} =$ 22) $\frac{1}{4} \times \frac{4}{5} =$

23) $\frac{1}{3} \times \frac{4}{5} =$ 24) $\frac{3}{4} \div \frac{1}{2} =$

25) $\frac{2}{3} \times \frac{1}{2} =$ 26) $\frac{1}{5} \times \frac{2}{3} =$

27) $\frac{1}{9} \div \frac{1}{2} =$ 28) $\frac{1}{7} \div \frac{2}{5} =$

29) $\frac{2}{3} \div \frac{1}{2} =$ 30) $\frac{1}{3} \times \frac{1}{3} =$

1) $\frac{2}{3} \times \frac{4}{5} =$

2) $\frac{1}{2} \times \frac{1}{2} =$

3) $\frac{9}{10} \div \frac{4}{5} =$

4) $\frac{4}{5} \div \frac{1}{4} =$

5) $\frac{1}{2} \div \frac{1}{2} =$

6) $\frac{4}{5} \times \frac{7}{9} =$

7) $\frac{1}{2} \times \frac{2}{5} =$

8) $\frac{3}{5} \div \frac{1}{5} =$

9) $\frac{2}{5} \times \frac{8}{9} =$

10) $\frac{8}{9} \div \frac{1}{2} =$

11) $\frac{1}{4} \times 1 =$

12) $1 \div \frac{4}{7} =$

13) $\frac{1}{4} \div \frac{1}{2} =$

14) $\frac{1}{3} \div \frac{1}{2} =$

15) $\frac{1}{6} \times \frac{3}{4} =$

52/62

16) $\frac{1}{2} \times \frac{7}{9} =$

17) $\frac{2}{3} \div \frac{5}{9} =$

18) $\frac{2}{5} \times \frac{1}{2} =$

19) $\frac{1}{3} \times \frac{1}{4} =$

20) $\frac{6}{7} \div \frac{1}{5} =$

21) $\frac{1}{4} \times \frac{5}{7} =$

22) $\frac{3}{4} \times \frac{1}{7} =$

23) $\frac{1}{2} \div \frac{4}{9} =$

24) $\frac{1}{4} \div \frac{3}{8} =$

25) $\frac{2}{5} \times \frac{1}{2} =$

26) $\frac{1}{3} \times \frac{1}{2} =$

27) $\frac{1}{4} \div \frac{7}{9} =$

28) $\frac{1}{2} \div \frac{1}{6} =$

29) $\frac{4}{5} \times \frac{2}{3} =$

30) $\frac{3}{7} \div \frac{2}{3} =$

1) $\frac{1}{2} \times \frac{1}{8} =$

2) $\frac{3}{8} \div \frac{7}{9} =$

3) $\frac{1}{10} \div \frac{1}{7} =$

4) $\frac{4}{7} \times \frac{5}{8} =$

5) $\frac{3}{4} \div \frac{1}{2} =$

6) $\frac{2}{5} \times \frac{7}{8} =$

7) $\frac{1}{4} \div \frac{1}{7} =$

8) $\frac{2}{7} \times \frac{2}{3} =$

9) $\frac{1}{2} \times \frac{3}{10} =$

10) $\frac{2}{3} \div \frac{3}{10} =$

11) $\frac{1}{2} \times \frac{7}{8} =$

12) $\frac{1}{2} \div \frac{4}{9} =$

13) $\frac{1}{8} \times \frac{1}{2} =$

14) $\frac{1}{3} \div \frac{1}{2} =$

15) $\frac{6}{7} \div \frac{1}{2} =$

16) $\frac{4}{5} \times \frac{4}{9} =$

17) $\frac{2}{5} \times \frac{1}{3} =$

18) $\frac{1}{5} \times \frac{2}{7} =$

19) $\frac{2}{3} \div \frac{1}{3} =$

20) $\frac{8}{9} \div \frac{2}{3} =$

21) $\frac{1}{9} \div \frac{2}{9} =$

22) $\frac{1}{3} \times \frac{1}{2} =$

23) $\frac{1}{2} \times \frac{3}{5} =$

24) $\frac{1}{5} \div \frac{2}{5} =$

25) $\frac{8}{9} \div \frac{1}{2} =$

26) $\frac{1}{2} \times \frac{1}{2} =$

27) $\frac{1}{2} \div \frac{3}{4} =$

28) $1 \times \frac{5}{9} =$

29) $\frac{4}{7} \times \frac{1}{3} =$

30) $\frac{2}{5} \div \frac{2}{7} =$

53/62

1) $\frac{4}{7} \div \frac{1}{2} =$ 2) $\frac{1}{2} \times \frac{3}{5} =$

3) $\frac{2}{5} \div \frac{2}{7} =$ 4) $\frac{2}{5} \times \frac{1}{8} =$

5) $\frac{1}{4} \times \frac{3}{10} =$ 6) $\frac{5}{6} \div \frac{1}{2} =$

7) $\frac{6}{7} \times \frac{1}{7} =$ 8) $\frac{3}{4} \div \frac{1}{8} =$

9) $\frac{1}{10} \div \frac{2}{3} =$ 10) $\frac{3}{5} \times \frac{1}{5} =$

11) $\frac{1}{6} \times \frac{1}{6} =$ 12) $\frac{5}{7} \div \frac{1}{2} =$

13) $\frac{1}{5} \times \frac{5}{8} =$ 14) $\frac{1}{2} \div \frac{5}{8} =$

15) $\frac{3}{7} \times \frac{1}{6} =$ 16) $\frac{1}{2} \div \frac{1}{2} =$

54/62

17) $\frac{1}{2} \times \frac{2}{3} =$ 18) $\frac{2}{7} \div \frac{4}{7} =$

19) $\frac{1}{2} \div \frac{1}{3} =$ 20) $\frac{4}{9} \times \frac{3}{4} =$

21) $\frac{1}{4} \times \frac{5}{9} =$ 22) $\frac{1}{2} \div \frac{3}{4} =$

23) $\frac{7}{10} \div \frac{3}{4} =$ 24) $\frac{2}{3} \times \frac{1}{3} =$

25) $\frac{4}{5} \div \frac{2}{3} =$ 26) $\frac{1}{4} \div \frac{3}{5} =$

27) $\frac{3}{4} \times \frac{1}{3} =$ 28) $\frac{2}{5} \times \frac{3}{4} =$

29) $\frac{1}{9} \div \frac{1}{5} =$ 30) $\frac{2}{3} \div \frac{1}{7} =$

1) $\frac{5}{8} \times \frac{3}{10} =$

2) $\frac{2}{3} \times \frac{1}{7} =$

3) $\frac{1}{5} \div \frac{3}{5} =$

4) $\frac{1}{3} \div \frac{1}{3} =$

5) $\frac{1}{8} \div \frac{2}{7} =$

6) $\frac{1}{2} \times \frac{3}{8} =$

7) $\frac{1}{2} \div \frac{5}{8} =$

8) $\frac{3}{4} \times \frac{2}{7} =$

9) $\frac{1}{3} \div \frac{3}{5} =$

10) $\frac{1}{2} \times \frac{1}{2} =$

11) $\frac{1}{5} \times \frac{4}{9} =$

12) $\frac{2}{3} \div \frac{2}{5} =$

13) $\frac{1}{2} \times \frac{1}{3} =$

14) $\frac{2}{3} \div \frac{7}{8} =$

15) $\frac{2}{3} \times \frac{1}{2} =$

16) $\frac{1}{8} \div \frac{1}{2} =$

17) $\frac{1}{4} \div \frac{3}{4} =$

18) $\frac{1}{2} \times \frac{1}{2} =$

19) $\frac{3}{5} \div \frac{1}{6} =$

20) $\frac{5}{8} \times \frac{1}{2} =$

21) $\frac{1}{2} \times \frac{1}{4} =$

22) $\frac{8}{9} \div \frac{1}{7} =$

23) $\frac{1}{9} \times \frac{1}{6} =$

24) $\frac{1}{6} \div \frac{5}{8} =$

25) $\frac{1}{2} \div \frac{1}{2} =$

26) $\frac{3}{5} \times \frac{1}{2} =$

27) $\frac{1}{3} \times \frac{1}{2} =$

28) $\frac{1}{2} \div \frac{1}{5} =$

29) $\frac{2}{5} \div \frac{3}{4} =$

30) $\frac{1}{4} \times \frac{3}{4} =$

55/62

1) $\frac{4}{2} \times \frac{1}{2} =$

2) $\frac{5}{2} \div \frac{9}{2} =$

3) $\frac{4}{7} \div \frac{14}{7} =$

4) $\frac{12}{5} \times \frac{13}{5} =$

5) $\frac{19}{4} \times \frac{7}{4} =$

6) $\frac{16}{4} \div \frac{11}{4} =$

7) $\frac{26}{8} \div \frac{30}{8} =$

8) $\frac{5}{2} \times \frac{9}{2} =$

9) $\frac{4}{5} \div \frac{2}{5} =$

10) $\frac{3}{2} \times \frac{3}{2} =$

11) $\frac{13}{5} \div \frac{21}{5} =$

12) $\frac{19}{9} \times \frac{1}{9} =$

13) $\frac{9}{6} \div \frac{8}{6} =$

14) $\frac{32}{7} \times \frac{12}{7} =$

15) $\frac{8}{7} \times \frac{12}{7} =$

56/62

16) $\frac{17}{7} \div \frac{9}{7} =$

17) $\frac{15}{3} \div \frac{8}{3} =$

18) $\frac{43}{9} \times \frac{28}{9} =$

19) $\frac{16}{7} \times \frac{26}{7} =$

20) $\frac{8}{9} \div \frac{1}{9} =$

21) $\frac{11}{6} \times \frac{11}{6} =$

22) $\frac{22}{5} \div \frac{9}{5} =$

23) $\frac{13}{3} \times \frac{10}{3} =$

24) $\frac{6}{7} \div \frac{29}{7} =$

25) $\frac{27}{8} \div \frac{16}{8} =$

26) $\frac{32}{7} \div \frac{4}{7} =$

27) $\frac{19}{10} \times \frac{9}{10} =$

28) $\frac{6}{5} \times \frac{3}{5} =$

29) $\frac{8}{9} \div \frac{37}{9} =$

30) $\frac{7}{7} \times \frac{23}{7} =$

1) $\frac{13}{6} \times \frac{13}{6} =$

2) $\frac{18}{7} \div \frac{24}{7} =$

3) $\frac{3}{4} \times \frac{7}{4} =$

4) $\frac{4}{3} \div \frac{7}{3} =$

5) $\frac{4}{2} \times \frac{1}{2} =$

6) $\frac{30}{8} \div \frac{26}{8} =$

7) $\frac{7}{4} \times \frac{13}{4} =$

8) $\frac{1}{10} \div \frac{2}{10} =$

9) $\frac{3}{3} \times \frac{1}{3} =$

10) $\frac{3}{8} \times \frac{18}{8} =$

11) $\frac{3}{3} \div \frac{2}{3} =$

12) $\frac{18}{10} \div \frac{39}{10} =$

13) $\frac{7}{3} \div \frac{13}{3} =$

14) $\frac{20}{7} \div \frac{28}{7} =$

15) $\frac{35}{9} \times \frac{10}{9} =$

16) $\frac{2}{3} \times \frac{9}{3} =$

17) $\frac{3}{2} \times \frac{11}{2} =$

18) $\frac{7}{3} \div \frac{13}{3} =$

19) $\frac{4}{9} \div \frac{19}{9} =$

20) $\frac{4}{2} \times \frac{9}{2} =$

21) $\frac{7}{9} \times \frac{7}{9} =$

22) $\frac{15}{6} \div \frac{2}{6} =$

23) $\frac{7}{2} \times \frac{6}{2} =$

24) $\frac{7}{6} \div \frac{16}{6} =$

25) $\frac{3}{9} \div \frac{36}{9} =$

26) $\frac{23}{5} \times \frac{18}{5} =$

27) $\frac{34}{7} \div \frac{32}{7} =$

28) $\frac{5}{7} \times \frac{8}{7} =$

29) $\frac{13}{9} \times \frac{35}{9} =$

30) $\frac{26}{6} \div \frac{1}{6} =$

57/62

1) $\frac{24}{6} \div \frac{14}{6} =$

2) $\frac{5}{3} \times \frac{10}{3} =$

3) $\frac{23}{10} \times \frac{14}{10} =$

4) $\frac{15}{4} \div \frac{14}{4} =$

5) $\frac{1}{4} \times \frac{14}{4} =$

6) $\frac{21}{10} \div \frac{3}{10} =$

7) $\frac{17}{6} \div \frac{10}{6} =$

8) $\frac{6}{4} \times \frac{13}{4} =$

9) $\frac{21}{5} \div \frac{19}{5} =$

10) $\frac{5}{2} \div \frac{5}{2} =$

11) $\frac{1}{5} \times \frac{15}{5} =$

12) $\frac{7}{2} \times \frac{8}{2} =$

13) $\frac{8}{3} \div \frac{9}{3} =$

14) $\frac{4}{6} \times \frac{23}{6} =$

15) $\frac{8}{6} \times \frac{24}{6} =$

58/62

16) $\frac{9}{9} \div \frac{39}{9} =$

17) $\frac{7}{4} \div \frac{6}{4} =$

18) $\frac{5}{10} \times \frac{48}{10} =$

19) $\frac{18}{4} \div \frac{14}{4} =$

20) $\frac{7}{4} \times \frac{15}{4} =$

21) $\frac{27}{9} \div \frac{14}{9} =$

22) $\frac{34}{7} \div \frac{4}{7} =$

23) $\frac{14}{4} \times \frac{13}{4} =$

24) $\frac{9}{10} \times \frac{35}{10} =$

25) $\frac{3}{2} \times \frac{2}{2} =$

26) $\frac{8}{7} \div \frac{31}{7} =$

27) $\frac{4}{8} \times \frac{29}{8} =$

28) $\frac{2}{3} \div \frac{2}{3} =$

29) $\frac{4}{6} \div \frac{26}{6} =$

30) $\frac{7}{9} \times \frac{12}{9} =$

1) $\frac{10}{4} \div \frac{16}{4} =$

2) $\frac{19}{6} \times \frac{2}{6} =$

3) $\frac{3}{3} \times \frac{7}{3} =$

4) $\frac{25}{5} \div \frac{18}{5} =$

5) $\frac{11}{4} \div \frac{10}{4} =$

6) $\frac{36}{8} \div \frac{25}{8} =$

7) $\frac{22}{5} \times \frac{18}{5} =$

8) $\frac{27}{9} \times \frac{5}{9} =$

9) $\frac{15}{5} \times \frac{12}{5} =$

10) $\frac{21}{4} \div \frac{17}{4} =$

11) $\frac{4}{6} \times \frac{2}{6} =$

12) $\frac{27}{8} \div \frac{3}{8} =$

13) $\frac{24}{8} \div \frac{33}{8} =$

14) $\frac{1}{2} \times \frac{1}{2} =$

15) $\frac{4}{2} \div \frac{3}{2} =$

16) $\frac{31}{6} \times \frac{7}{6} =$

17) $\frac{8}{2} \times \frac{5}{2} =$

18) $\frac{30}{9} \div \frac{19}{9} =$

19) $\frac{11}{4} \times \frac{20}{4} =$

20) $\frac{14}{3} \div \frac{5}{3} =$

21) $\frac{5}{2} \div \frac{11}{2} =$

22) $\frac{23}{6} \times \frac{4}{6} =$

23) $\frac{36}{9} \times \frac{16}{9} =$

24) $\frac{20}{10} \div \frac{4}{10} =$

25) $\frac{1}{2} \times \frac{7}{2} =$

26) $\frac{30}{10} \times \frac{45}{10} =$

27) $\frac{9}{3} \div \frac{1}{3} =$

28) $\frac{10}{8} \div \frac{2}{8} =$

29) $\frac{1}{2} \div \frac{7}{2} =$

30) $\frac{6}{8} \times \frac{1}{8} =$

59/62

1) $\frac{17}{10} \times \frac{8}{10} =$ 2) $\frac{11}{2} \times \frac{9}{2} =$

3) $\frac{33}{9} \div \frac{8}{9} =$ 4) $\frac{22}{5} \div \frac{17}{5} =$

5) $\frac{28}{7} \div \frac{15}{7} =$ 6) $\frac{41}{9} \times \frac{25}{9} =$

7) $\frac{19}{8} \div \frac{19}{8} =$ 8) $\frac{23}{8} \times \frac{34}{8} =$

9) $\frac{33}{7} \div \frac{17}{7} =$ 10) $\frac{1}{7} \times \frac{33}{7} =$

11) $\frac{41}{10} \times \frac{42}{10} =$ 12) $\frac{8}{3} \div \frac{11}{3} =$

13) $\frac{5}{10} \div \frac{21}{10} =$ 14) $\frac{20}{7} \times \frac{10}{7} =$

60/62

15) $\frac{21}{10} \times \frac{30}{10} =$ 16) $\frac{12}{4} \div \frac{7}{4} =$

17) $\frac{17}{4} \div \frac{20}{4} =$ 18) $\frac{13}{3} \times \frac{10}{3} =$

19) $\frac{13}{7} \times \frac{15}{7} =$ 20) $\frac{20}{10} \div \frac{31}{10} =$

21) $\frac{20}{8} \div \frac{30}{8} =$ 22) $\frac{14}{6} \times \frac{1}{6} =$

23) $\frac{11}{5} \times \frac{11}{5} =$ 24) $\frac{5}{2} \div \frac{5}{2} =$

25) $\frac{5}{3} \div \frac{11}{3} =$ 26) $\frac{5}{5} \times \frac{24}{5} =$

27) $\frac{2}{4} \times \frac{17}{4} =$ 28) $\frac{5}{2} \div \frac{3}{2} =$

29) $\frac{19}{8} \div \frac{40}{8} =$ 30) $\frac{28}{8} \div \frac{10}{8} =$

Answears

1) $\frac{1}{2} \times \frac{3}{4} = \frac{3}{8}$

2) $\frac{1}{4} \times \frac{2}{3} = \frac{1}{6}$

3) $\frac{1}{2} \times \frac{1}{2} = \frac{1}{4}$

4) $\frac{2}{5} \times \frac{1}{2} = \frac{1}{5}$

5) $\frac{1}{3} \times \frac{2}{3} = \frac{2}{9}$

6) $\frac{2}{3} \times \frac{2}{5} = \frac{4}{15}$

7) $\frac{2}{3} \times \frac{1}{5} = \frac{2}{15}$

8) $\frac{3}{4} \times \frac{1}{2} = \frac{3}{8}$

9) $\frac{1}{3} \times \frac{1}{4} = \frac{1}{12}$

10) $\frac{1}{2} \times \frac{1}{2} = \frac{1}{4}$

11) $\frac{1}{2} \times \frac{3}{4} = \frac{3}{8}$

12) $\frac{4}{5} \times \frac{2}{3} = \frac{8}{15}$

13) $\frac{1}{5} \times \frac{4}{5} = \frac{4}{25}$

14) $\frac{1}{2} \times \frac{1}{3} = \frac{1}{6}$

15) $\frac{1}{3} \times \frac{2}{3} = \frac{2}{9}$

16) $\frac{2}{3} \times \frac{1}{4} = \frac{1}{6}$

17) $\frac{1}{2} \times \frac{1}{2} = \frac{1}{4}$

18) $\frac{3}{4} \times \frac{1}{2} = \frac{3}{8}$

19) $\frac{1}{2} \times \frac{1}{4} = \frac{1}{8}$

20) $\frac{1}{3} \times \frac{1}{2} = \frac{1}{6}$

21) $\frac{1}{2} \times \frac{3}{4} = \frac{3}{8}$

22) $\frac{3}{5} \times \frac{3}{4} = \frac{9}{20}$

23) $\frac{1}{2} \times \frac{1}{4} = \frac{1}{8}$

24) $\frac{1}{5} \times \frac{1}{2} = \frac{1}{10}$

25) $\frac{3}{4} \times \frac{1}{3} = \frac{1}{4}$

26) $\frac{4}{5} \times \frac{3}{4} = \frac{3}{5}$

27) $\frac{1}{4} \times \frac{1}{2} = \frac{1}{8}$

28) $\frac{1}{3} \times \frac{1}{4} = \frac{1}{12}$

29) $\frac{2}{5} \times \frac{1}{2} = \frac{1}{5}$

30) $\frac{2}{3} \times \frac{1}{2} = \frac{1}{3}$

1/62

1) $\frac{2}{5} \times \frac{1}{3} = \frac{2}{15}$

2) $\frac{1}{2} \times \frac{1}{4} = \frac{1}{8}$

3) $\frac{2}{5} \times \frac{2}{3} = \frac{4}{15}$

4) $\frac{3}{4} \times \frac{3}{4} = \frac{9}{16}$

5) $\frac{2}{3} \times \frac{1}{2} = \frac{1}{3}$

6) $\frac{1}{2} \times \frac{1}{3} = \frac{1}{6}$

7) $\frac{1}{3} \times \frac{1}{3} = \frac{1}{9}$

8) $\frac{1}{5} \times \frac{1}{4} = \frac{1}{20}$

9) $\frac{2}{5} \times \frac{1}{2} = \frac{1}{5}$

10) $\frac{2}{3} \times \frac{1}{2} = \frac{1}{3}$

11) $\frac{1}{3} \times \frac{1}{2} = \frac{1}{6}$

12) $\frac{1}{2} \times \frac{1}{3} = \frac{1}{6}$

13) $\frac{4}{5} \times 1 = \frac{4}{5}$

14) $\frac{1}{3} \times \frac{3}{5} = \frac{1}{5}$

15) $\frac{1}{3} \times \frac{4}{5} = \frac{4}{15}$

2/62

16) $\frac{1}{4} \times \frac{1}{3} = \frac{1}{12}$

17) $\frac{3}{4} \times \frac{2}{3} = \frac{1}{2}$

18) $\frac{1}{2} \times \frac{1}{3} = \frac{1}{6}$

19) $\frac{1}{4} \times \frac{3}{4} = \frac{3}{16}$

20) $\frac{1}{2} \times \frac{1}{2} = \frac{1}{4}$

21) $\frac{1}{3} \times \frac{2}{3} = \frac{2}{9}$

22) $\frac{1}{3} \times \frac{1}{2} = \frac{1}{6}$

23) $\frac{3}{4} \times \frac{2}{3} = \frac{1}{2}$

24) $\frac{3}{5} \times \frac{2}{3} = \frac{2}{5}$

25) $\frac{1}{2} \times \frac{4}{5} = \frac{2}{5}$

26) $\frac{3}{4} \times \frac{1}{2} = \frac{3}{8}$

27) $\frac{2}{5} \times \frac{4}{5} = \frac{8}{25}$

28) $\frac{4}{5} \times \frac{1}{2} = \frac{2}{5}$

29) $\frac{1}{2} \times \frac{2}{3} = \frac{1}{3}$

30) $\frac{1}{3} \times \frac{3}{5} = \frac{1}{5}$

1) $\frac{1}{4} \times \frac{1}{2} = \frac{1}{8}$

2) $\frac{1}{5} \times \frac{3}{5} = \frac{3}{25}$

3) $\frac{3}{5} \times \frac{1}{5} = \frac{3}{25}$

4) $\frac{1}{2} \times \frac{1}{2} = \frac{1}{4}$

5) $\frac{1}{5} \times \frac{2}{3} = \frac{2}{15}$

6) $\frac{1}{3} \times \frac{1}{2} = \frac{1}{6}$

7) $\frac{2}{3} \times \frac{3}{4} = \frac{1}{2}$

8) $\frac{1}{2} \times \frac{1}{3} = \frac{1}{6}$

9) $\frac{1}{4} \times 1 = \frac{1}{4}$

10) $\frac{2}{3} \times \frac{1}{2} = \frac{1}{3}$

11) $\frac{1}{3} \times \frac{4}{5} = \frac{4}{15}$

12) $1 \times \frac{1}{3} = \frac{1}{3}$

13) $\frac{2}{5} \times \frac{2}{5} = \frac{4}{25}$

14) $\frac{1}{2} \times \frac{1}{3} = \frac{1}{6}$

15) $\frac{2}{3} \times \frac{2}{3} = \frac{4}{9}$

16) $\frac{1}{2} \times \frac{2}{3} = \frac{1}{3}$

17) $1 \times \frac{3}{4} = \frac{3}{4}$

18) $\frac{1}{4} \times \frac{1}{2} = \frac{1}{8}$

19) $\frac{1}{2} \times \frac{3}{4} = \frac{3}{8}$

20) $\frac{4}{5} \times \frac{1}{3} = \frac{4}{15}$

21) $\frac{4}{5} \times \frac{3}{5} = \frac{12}{25}$

22) $\frac{3}{4} \times \frac{2}{5} = \frac{3}{10}$

23) $\frac{1}{3} \times \frac{1}{2} = \frac{1}{6}$

24) $\frac{1}{2} \times \frac{3}{4} = \frac{3}{8}$

25) $\frac{3}{4} \times \frac{1}{2} = \frac{3}{8}$

26) $\frac{1}{2} \times \frac{1}{2} = \frac{1}{4}$

27) $1 \times \frac{3}{5} = \frac{3}{5}$

28) $\frac{1}{2} \times \frac{1}{4} = \frac{1}{8}$

29) $\frac{4}{5} \times \frac{1}{2} = \frac{2}{5}$

30) $\frac{2}{3} \times \frac{3}{4} = \frac{1}{2}$

1) $\frac{1}{2}$ x $\frac{2}{3}$ = $\frac{1}{3}$

2) $\frac{3}{5}$ x $\frac{3}{5}$ = $\frac{9}{25}$

3) $\frac{1}{3}$ x $\frac{2}{3}$ = $\frac{2}{9}$

4) $\frac{2}{3}$ x $\frac{3}{5}$ = $\frac{2}{5}$

5) $\frac{4}{5}$ x $\frac{2}{5}$ = $\frac{8}{25}$

6) $\frac{1}{3}$ x $\frac{1}{2}$ = $\frac{1}{6}$

7) $\frac{1}{2}$ x $\frac{1}{3}$ = $\frac{1}{6}$

8) $\frac{1}{3}$ x 1 = $\frac{1}{3}$

9) $\frac{1}{2}$ x $\frac{3}{4}$ = $\frac{3}{8}$

10) $\frac{1}{4}$ x $\frac{1}{2}$ = $\frac{1}{8}$

11) $\frac{1}{3}$ x $\frac{1}{2}$ = $\frac{1}{6}$

12) $\frac{1}{2}$ x $\frac{4}{5}$ = $\frac{2}{5}$

13) $\frac{3}{5}$ x $\frac{2}{3}$ = $\frac{2}{5}$

14) $\frac{3}{4}$ x $\frac{2}{3}$ = $\frac{1}{2}$

15) $\frac{1}{2}$ x $\frac{1}{4}$ = $\frac{1}{8}$

16) $\frac{1}{4}$ x $\frac{3}{4}$ = $\frac{3}{16}$

17) $\frac{1}{2}$ x $\frac{1}{3}$ = $\frac{1}{6}$

18) $\frac{3}{5}$ x $\frac{1}{3}$ = $\frac{1}{5}$

19) $\frac{1}{2}$ x $\frac{3}{5}$ = $\frac{3}{10}$

20) $\frac{2}{3}$ x $\frac{1}{2}$ = $\frac{1}{3}$

21) $\frac{1}{2}$ x $\frac{1}{2}$ = $\frac{1}{4}$

22) $\frac{2}{3}$ x $\frac{1}{2}$ = $\frac{1}{3}$

23) $\frac{2}{3}$ x $\frac{2}{5}$ = $\frac{4}{15}$

24) $\frac{3}{4}$ x $\frac{3}{4}$ = $\frac{9}{16}$

25) $\frac{1}{2}$ x $\frac{2}{5}$ = $\frac{1}{5}$

26) $\frac{2}{5}$ x $\frac{1}{3}$ = $\frac{2}{15}$

27) $\frac{1}{3}$ x $\frac{3}{4}$ = $\frac{1}{4}$

28) $\frac{1}{2}$ x $\frac{1}{2}$ = $\frac{1}{4}$

29) $\frac{1}{5}$ x $\frac{1}{3}$ = $\frac{1}{15}$

30) $\frac{1}{5}$ x $\frac{3}{5}$ = $\frac{3}{25}$

4/62

1) $\frac{1}{2} \times \frac{1}{5} = \frac{1}{10}$ 2) $\frac{3}{4} \times \frac{1}{3} = \frac{1}{4}$

3) $\frac{1}{2} \times \frac{2}{3} = \frac{1}{3}$ 4) $\frac{1}{2} \times \frac{3}{5} = \frac{3}{10}$

5) $\frac{2}{3} \times \frac{1}{2} = \frac{1}{3}$ 6) $\frac{3}{4} \times \frac{1}{2} = \frac{3}{8}$

7) $\frac{1}{3} \times \frac{2}{3} = \frac{2}{9}$ 8) $\frac{4}{5} \times \frac{2}{3} = \frac{8}{15}$

9) $\frac{1}{5} \times \frac{1}{5} = \frac{1}{25}$ 10) $\frac{3}{4} \times \frac{1}{2} = \frac{3}{8}$

11) $\frac{2}{5} \times \frac{2}{3} = \frac{4}{15}$ 12) $\frac{3}{4} \times \frac{1}{2} = \frac{3}{8}$

13) $\frac{3}{5} \times \frac{2}{5} = \frac{6}{25}$ 14) $\frac{3}{5} \times \frac{1}{2} = \frac{3}{10}$

15) $\frac{1}{3} \times \frac{2}{3} = \frac{2}{9}$ 16) $\frac{1}{2} \times \frac{3}{5} = \frac{3}{10}$

17) $\frac{2}{3} \times \frac{2}{3} = \frac{4}{9}$ 18) $\frac{2}{3} \times \frac{4}{5} = \frac{8}{15}$

19) $\frac{1}{3} \times \frac{1}{2} = \frac{1}{6}$ 20) $\frac{1}{4} \times \frac{1}{3} = \frac{1}{12}$

21) $\frac{1}{2} \times \frac{3}{4} = \frac{3}{8}$ 22) $\frac{1}{5} \times \frac{1}{5} = \frac{1}{25}$

23) $\frac{1}{4} \times \frac{3}{5} = \frac{3}{20}$ 24) $\frac{2}{5} \times \frac{1}{5} = \frac{2}{25}$

25) $\frac{3}{5} \times 1 = \frac{3}{5}$ 26) $\frac{3}{4} \times \frac{3}{4} = \frac{9}{16}$

27) $\frac{1}{3} \times \frac{1}{5} = \frac{1}{15}$ 28) $\frac{1}{2} \times \frac{4}{5} = \frac{2}{5}$

29) $\frac{1}{2} \times \frac{1}{4} = \frac{1}{8}$ 30) $\frac{1}{3} \times \frac{1}{2} = \frac{1}{6}$

5/62

1) $\frac{1}{5}$ x $\frac{4}{3}$ = $\frac{4}{15}$

2) $\frac{13}{7}$ x $\frac{11}{3}$ = $\frac{143}{21}$ **or** $6\frac{17}{21}$

3) 4 x $\frac{1}{3}$ = $\frac{4}{3}$ **or** $1\frac{1}{3}$

4) $\frac{10}{7}$ x 2 = $\frac{20}{7}$ **or** $2\frac{6}{7}$

5) $\frac{4}{5}$ x $\frac{3}{2}$ = $\frac{6}{5}$ **or** $1\frac{1}{5}$

6) $\frac{8}{7}$ x $\frac{9}{2}$ = $\frac{36}{7}$ **or** $5\frac{1}{7}$

7) 2 x $\frac{2}{3}$ = $\frac{4}{3}$ **or** $1\frac{1}{3}$

8) $\frac{21}{8}$ x 1 = $\frac{21}{8}$ **or** $2\frac{5}{8}$

9) $\frac{6}{5}$ x 3 = $\frac{18}{5}$ **or** $3\frac{3}{5}$

10) $\frac{11}{4}$ x $\frac{7}{3}$ = $\frac{77}{12}$ **or** $6\frac{5}{12}$

11) $\frac{35}{8}$ x 4 = $\frac{35}{2}$ **or** $17\frac{1}{2}$

12) $\frac{1}{4}$ x $\frac{9}{2}$ = $\frac{9}{8}$ **or** $1\frac{1}{8}$

13) $\frac{3}{2}$ x 2 = **3**

14) $\frac{4}{3}$ x $\frac{9}{2}$ = **6**

15) $\frac{3}{4}$ x $\frac{5}{2}$ = $\frac{15}{8}$ **or** $1\frac{7}{8}$

6/62

16) $\frac{9}{2}$ x $\frac{5}{4}$ = $\frac{45}{8}$ **or** $5\frac{5}{8}$

17) $\frac{3}{7}$ x 2 = $\frac{6}{7}$

18) $\frac{13}{5}$ x $\frac{9}{2}$ = $\frac{117}{10}$ **or** $11\frac{7}{10}$

19) 1 x $\frac{4}{3}$ = $\frac{4}{3}$ **or** $1\frac{1}{3}$

20) $\frac{7}{2}$ x $\frac{9}{2}$ = $\frac{63}{4}$ **or** $15\frac{3}{4}$

21) $\frac{9}{4}$ x $\frac{15}{4}$ = $\frac{135}{16}$ **or** $8\frac{7}{16}$

22) $\frac{11}{5}$ x $\frac{5}{4}$ = $\frac{11}{4}$ **or** $2\frac{3}{4}$

23) $\frac{13}{5}$ x $\frac{9}{2}$ = $\frac{117}{10}$ **or** $11\frac{7}{10}$

24) $\frac{29}{6}$ x $\frac{1}{5}$ = $\frac{29}{30}$

25) $\frac{23}{6}$ x $\frac{7}{3}$ = $\frac{161}{18}$ **or** $8\frac{17}{18}$

26) $\frac{5}{2}$ x $\frac{19}{5}$ = $\frac{19}{2}$ **or** $9\frac{1}{2}$

27) 2 x $\frac{5}{2}$ = **5**

28) $\frac{1}{2}$ x $\frac{2}{5}$ = $\frac{1}{5}$

29) 4 x $\frac{9}{2}$ = **18**

30) $\frac{25}{6}$ x $\frac{13}{5}$ = $\frac{65}{6}$ **or** $10\frac{5}{6}$

1) $\frac{19}{7} \times \frac{11}{4} = \frac{209}{28}$ **or** $7\frac{13}{28}$

2) $\frac{11}{4} \times \frac{11}{3} = \frac{121}{12}$ **or** $10\frac{1}{12}$

3) $4 \times \frac{24}{5} = \frac{96}{5}$ **or** $19\frac{1}{5}$

4) $\frac{24}{5} \times 5 =$ **24**

5) $\frac{5}{2} \times \frac{4}{3} = \frac{10}{3}$ **or** $3\frac{1}{3}$

6) $\frac{19}{4} \times 5 = \frac{95}{4}$ **or** $23\frac{3}{4}$

7) $\frac{3}{2} \times 4 =$ **6**

8) $\frac{2}{5} \times 4 = \frac{8}{5}$ **or** $1\frac{3}{5}$

9) $\frac{16}{5} \times \frac{4}{3} = \frac{64}{15}$ **or** $4\frac{4}{15}$

10) $\frac{1}{3} \times 2 = \frac{2}{3}$

11) $\frac{10}{7} \times \frac{13}{5} = \frac{26}{7}$ **or** $3\frac{5}{7}$

12) $\frac{26}{7} \times 3 = \frac{78}{7}$ **or** $11\frac{1}{7}$

13) $\frac{21}{5} \times \frac{1}{2} = \frac{21}{10}$ **or** $2\frac{1}{10}$

14) $\frac{17}{4} \times \frac{7}{5} = \frac{119}{20}$ **or** $5\frac{19}{20}$

15) $\frac{1}{4} \times \frac{23}{5} = \frac{23}{20}$ **or** $1\frac{3}{20}$

16) $\frac{3}{7} \times 1 = \frac{3}{7}$

7/62

17) $\frac{34}{7} \times \frac{13}{3} = \frac{442}{21}$ **or** $21\frac{1}{21}$

18) $\frac{13}{4} \times 4 =$ **13**

19) $\frac{7}{2} \times 2 =$ **7**

20) $\frac{7}{6} \times \frac{15}{4} = \frac{35}{8}$ **or** $4\frac{3}{8}$

21) $5 \times \frac{2}{3} = \frac{10}{3}$ **or** $3\frac{1}{3}$

22) $\frac{27}{7} \times \frac{1}{4} = \frac{27}{28}$

23) $\frac{13}{3} \times \frac{23}{5} = \frac{299}{15}$ **or** $19\frac{14}{15}$

24) $5 \times \frac{3}{4} = \frac{15}{4}$ **or** $3\frac{3}{4}$

25) $5 \times \frac{14}{3} = \frac{70}{3}$ **or** $23\frac{1}{3}$

26) $\frac{13}{5} \times \frac{7}{2} = \frac{91}{10}$ **or** $9\frac{1}{10}$

27) $\frac{3}{4} \times \frac{4}{5} = \frac{3}{5}$

28) $\frac{31}{7} \times \frac{14}{3} = \frac{62}{3}$ **or** $20\frac{2}{3}$

29) $\frac{21}{5} \times \frac{7}{3} = \frac{49}{5}$ **or** $9\frac{4}{5}$

30) $\frac{1}{2} \times 2 =$ **1**

1) $\frac{3}{4}$ x 5 = $\frac{15}{4}$ **or** $3\frac{3}{4}$

2) $\frac{5}{2}$ x $\frac{10}{3}$ = $\frac{25}{3}$ **or** $8\frac{1}{3}$

3) $\frac{8}{7}$ x $\frac{22}{5}$ = $\frac{176}{35}$ **or** $5\frac{1}{35}$

4) $\frac{9}{4}$ x $\frac{9}{2}$ = $\frac{81}{8}$ **or** $10\frac{1}{8}$

5) $\frac{19}{7}$ x $\frac{14}{5}$ = $\frac{38}{5}$ **or** $7\frac{3}{5}$

6) $\frac{21}{5}$ x $\frac{13}{4}$ = $\frac{273}{20}$ **or** $13\frac{13}{20}$

7) $\frac{17}{4}$ x $\frac{13}{3}$ = $\frac{221}{12}$ **or** $18\frac{5}{12}$

8) $\frac{5}{2}$ x $\frac{4}{3}$ = $\frac{10}{3}$ **or** $3\frac{1}{3}$

9) $\frac{39}{8}$ x $\frac{6}{5}$ = $\frac{117}{20}$ **or** $5\frac{17}{20}$

10) $\frac{22}{5}$ x $\frac{7}{3}$ = $\frac{154}{15}$ **or** $10\frac{4}{15}$

11) $\frac{13}{3}$ x 4 = $\frac{52}{3}$ **or** $17\frac{1}{3}$

12) $\frac{9}{8}$ x 2 = $\frac{9}{4}$ **or** $2\frac{1}{4}$

13) $\frac{8}{3}$ x $\frac{2}{3}$ = $\frac{16}{9}$ **or** $1\frac{7}{9}$

14) $\frac{4}{3}$ x $\frac{2}{3}$ = $\frac{8}{9}$

15) $\frac{5}{2}$ x $\frac{4}{3}$ = $\frac{10}{3}$ **or** $3\frac{1}{3}$

8/62

16) $\frac{7}{4}$ x $\frac{18}{5}$ = $\frac{63}{10}$ **or** $6\frac{3}{10}$

17) $\frac{16}{5}$ x $\frac{16}{3}$ = $\frac{256}{15}$ **or** $17\frac{1}{15}$

18) $\frac{3}{7}$ x $\frac{5}{4}$ = $\frac{15}{28}$

19) 1 x $\frac{13}{3}$ = $\frac{13}{3}$ **or** $4\frac{1}{3}$

20) $\frac{9}{4}$ x $\frac{9}{2}$ = $\frac{81}{8}$ **or** $10\frac{1}{8}$

21) $\frac{9}{4}$ x 3 = $\frac{27}{4}$ **or** $6\frac{3}{4}$

22) $\frac{13}{4}$ x $\frac{5}{4}$ = $\frac{65}{16}$ **or** $4\frac{1}{16}$

23) $\frac{17}{6}$ x 5 = $\frac{85}{6}$ **or** $14\frac{1}{6}$

24) 2 x $\frac{2}{3}$ = $\frac{4}{3}$ **or** $1\frac{1}{3}$

25) $\frac{7}{2}$ x $\frac{11}{4}$ = $\frac{77}{8}$ **or** $9\frac{5}{8}$

26) $\frac{1}{2}$ x 2 = **1**

27) 4 x $\frac{2}{3}$ = $\frac{8}{3}$ **or** $2\frac{2}{3}$

28) $\frac{9}{2}$ x $\frac{23}{5}$ = $\frac{207}{10}$ **or** $20\frac{7}{10}$

29) $\frac{3}{2}$ x $\frac{3}{4}$ = $\frac{9}{8}$ **or** $1\frac{1}{8}$

30) $\frac{32}{7}$ x 1 = $\frac{32}{7}$ **or** $4\frac{4}{7}$

1) $\frac{8}{3}$ x $\frac{13}{5}$ = $\frac{104}{15}$ **or** $6\frac{14}{15}$

2) $\frac{9}{2}$ x $\frac{23}{5}$ = $\frac{207}{10}$ **or** $20\frac{7}{10}$

3) $\frac{7}{2}$ x 5 = $\frac{35}{2}$ **or** $17\frac{1}{2}$

4) $\frac{6}{5}$ x $\frac{5}{2}$ = **3**

5) $\frac{3}{7}$ x 3 = $\frac{9}{7}$ **or** $1\frac{2}{7}$

6) $\frac{15}{4}$ x $\frac{8}{5}$ = **6**

7) $\frac{2}{3}$ x 4 = $\frac{8}{3}$ **or** $2\frac{2}{3}$

8) $\frac{7}{2}$ x $\frac{7}{3}$ = $\frac{49}{6}$ **or** $8\frac{1}{6}$

9) $\frac{4}{3}$ x $\frac{5}{2}$ = $\frac{10}{3}$ **or** $3\frac{1}{3}$

10) $\frac{1}{2}$ x $\frac{9}{2}$ = $\frac{9}{4}$ **or** $2\frac{1}{4}$

11) $\frac{9}{2}$ x 5 = $\frac{45}{2}$ **or** $22\frac{1}{2}$

12) $\frac{17}{7}$ x $\frac{1}{3}$ = $\frac{17}{21}$

13) $\frac{5}{2}$ x $\frac{3}{5}$ = $\frac{3}{2}$ **or** $1\frac{1}{2}$

14) $\frac{6}{5}$ x $\frac{13}{3}$ = $\frac{26}{5}$ **or** $5\frac{1}{5}$

15) 3 x $\frac{1}{3}$ = **1**

16) $\frac{22}{7}$ x $\frac{4}{3}$ = $\frac{88}{21}$ **or** $4\frac{4}{21}$

17) $\frac{3}{2}$ x $\frac{5}{2}$ = $\frac{15}{4}$ **or** $3\frac{3}{4}$

18) $\frac{1}{4}$ x 1 = $\frac{1}{4}$

19) $\frac{22}{7}$ x $\frac{11}{2}$ = $\frac{121}{7}$ **or** $17\frac{2}{7}$

20) $\frac{17}{4}$ x $\frac{3}{2}$ = $\frac{51}{8}$ **or** $6\frac{3}{8}$

21) $\frac{11}{2}$ x $\frac{9}{2}$ = $\frac{99}{4}$ **or** $24\frac{3}{4}$

22) $\frac{13}{6}$ x 3 = $\frac{13}{2}$ **or** $6\frac{1}{2}$

23) $\frac{11}{3}$ x 4 = $\frac{44}{3}$ **or** $14\frac{2}{3}$

24) $\frac{7}{2}$ x $\frac{5}{2}$ = $\frac{35}{4}$ **or** $8\frac{3}{4}$

25) 3 x $\frac{2}{3}$ = **2**

26) $\frac{24}{7}$ x $\frac{13}{5}$ = $\frac{312}{35}$ **or** $8\frac{32}{35}$

27) $\frac{11}{2}$ x $\frac{16}{3}$ = $\frac{88}{3}$ **or** $29\frac{1}{3}$

28) $\frac{16}{7}$ x $\frac{15}{4}$ = $\frac{60}{7}$ **or** $8\frac{4}{7}$

29) $\frac{10}{3}$ x $\frac{3}{2}$ = **5**

30) 3 x $\frac{13}{4}$ = $\frac{39}{4}$ **or** $9\frac{3}{4}$

9/62

1) $\frac{11}{3} \times \frac{3}{4} = \frac{11}{4}$ **or** $2\frac{3}{4}$

2) $\frac{2}{3} \times \frac{9}{2} =$ **3**

3) $5 \times \frac{5}{4} = \frac{25}{4}$ **or** $6\frac{1}{4}$

4) $\frac{7}{3} \times \frac{4}{3} = \frac{28}{9}$ **or** $3\frac{1}{9}$

5) $\frac{17}{5} \times \frac{9}{2} = \frac{153}{10}$ **or** $15\frac{3}{10}$

6) $\frac{35}{8} \times \frac{12}{5} = \frac{21}{2}$ **or** $10\frac{1}{2}$

7) $\frac{4}{3} \times \frac{12}{5} = \frac{16}{5}$ **or** $3\frac{1}{5}$

8) $\frac{13}{3} \times \frac{11}{5} = \frac{143}{15}$ **or** $9\frac{8}{15}$

9) $3 \times \frac{7}{2} = \frac{21}{2}$ **or** $10\frac{1}{2}$

10) $\frac{3}{8} \times \frac{9}{2} = \frac{27}{16}$ **or** $1\frac{11}{16}$

11) $\frac{5}{4} \times 4 =$ **5**

12) $\frac{3}{2} \times \frac{1}{2} = \frac{3}{4}$

13) $2 \times \frac{9}{2} =$ **9**

14) $\frac{5}{8} \times 2 = \frac{5}{4}$ **or** $1\frac{1}{4}$

15) $\frac{1}{2} \times 5 = \frac{5}{2}$ **or** $2\frac{1}{2}$

10/62

16) $\frac{1}{8} \times \frac{1}{2} = \frac{1}{16}$

17) $\frac{17}{4} \times \frac{11}{2} = \frac{187}{8}$ **or** $23\frac{3}{8}$

18) $\frac{9}{2} \times 3 = \frac{27}{2}$ **or** $13\frac{1}{2}$

19) $\frac{18}{5} \times \frac{9}{4} = \frac{81}{10}$ **or** $8\frac{1}{10}$

20) $\frac{26}{7} \times 1 = \frac{26}{7}$ **or** $3\frac{5}{7}$

21) $\frac{2}{3} \times 1 = \frac{2}{3}$

22) $\frac{31}{6} \times \frac{7}{2} = \frac{217}{12}$ **or** $18\frac{1}{12}$

23) $\frac{14}{3} \times \frac{11}{5} = \frac{154}{15}$ **or** $10\frac{4}{15}$

24) $\frac{1}{3} \times \frac{3}{4} = \frac{1}{4}$

25) $\frac{1}{3} \times \frac{7}{4} = \frac{7}{12}$

26) $\frac{9}{8} \times 5 = \frac{45}{8}$ **or** $5\frac{5}{8}$

27) $\frac{19}{5} \times 1 = \frac{19}{5}$ **or** $3\frac{4}{5}$

28) $\frac{4}{3} \times \frac{3}{5} = \frac{4}{5}$

29) $\frac{5}{2} \times \frac{11}{4} = \frac{55}{8}$ **or** $6\frac{7}{8}$

30) $\frac{17}{7} \times \frac{2}{3} = \frac{34}{21}$ **or** $1\frac{13}{21}$

1) $\frac{16}{5}$ x $\frac{17}{4}$ = $\frac{68}{5}$ **or** $13\frac{3}{5}$

2) $\frac{7}{4}$ x $\frac{1}{2}$ = $\frac{7}{8}$

3) $\frac{10}{3}$ x $\frac{4}{3}$ = $\frac{40}{9}$ **or** $4\frac{4}{9}$

4) $\frac{1}{4}$ x 5 = $\frac{5}{4}$ **or** $1\frac{1}{4}$

5) $\frac{2}{7}$ x $\frac{17}{4}$ = $\frac{17}{14}$ **or** $1\frac{3}{14}$

6) $\frac{15}{7}$ x $\frac{13}{5}$ = $\frac{39}{7}$ **or** $5\frac{4}{7}$

7) $\frac{7}{4}$ x $\frac{5}{2}$ = $\frac{35}{8}$ **or** $4\frac{3}{8}$

8) $\frac{4}{3}$ x $\frac{2}{3}$ = $\frac{8}{9}$

9) $\frac{11}{4}$ x $\frac{18}{5}$ = $\frac{99}{10}$ **or** $9\frac{9}{10}$

10) $\frac{9}{2}$ x 5 = $\frac{45}{2}$ **or** $22\frac{1}{2}$

11) 5 x $\frac{11}{5}$ = **11**

12) $\frac{5}{2}$ x 3 = $\frac{15}{2}$ **or** $7\frac{1}{2}$

13) $\frac{2}{3}$ x $\frac{14}{3}$ = $\frac{28}{9}$ **or** $3\frac{1}{9}$

14) $\frac{7}{3}$ x 3 = **7**

15) $\frac{10}{3}$ x 1 = $\frac{10}{3}$ **or** $3\frac{1}{3}$

11/62

16) $\frac{7}{3}$ x $\frac{8}{3}$ = $\frac{56}{9}$ **or** $6\frac{2}{9}$

17) 5 x $\frac{3}{4}$ = $\frac{15}{4}$ **or** $3\frac{3}{4}$

18) $\frac{2}{3}$ x $\frac{1}{2}$ = $\frac{1}{3}$

19) $\frac{17}{4}$ x $\frac{7}{3}$ = $\frac{119}{12}$ **or** $9\frac{11}{12}$

20) $\frac{6}{5}$ x $\frac{9}{2}$ = $\frac{27}{5}$ **or** $5\frac{2}{5}$

21) $\frac{20}{7}$ x 1 = $\frac{20}{7}$ **or** $2\frac{6}{7}$

22) $\frac{13}{8}$ x 5 = $\frac{65}{8}$ **or** $8\frac{1}{8}$

23) $\frac{13}{4}$ x 5 = $\frac{65}{4}$ **or** $16\frac{1}{4}$

24) 5 x $\frac{11}{3}$ = $\frac{55}{3}$ **or** $18\frac{1}{3}$

25) 4 x $\frac{11}{3}$ = $\frac{44}{3}$ **or** $14\frac{2}{3}$

26) $\frac{1}{3}$ x $\frac{15}{4}$ = $\frac{5}{4}$ **or** $1\frac{1}{4}$

27) 5 x $\frac{2}{3}$ = $\frac{10}{3}$ **or** $3\frac{1}{3}$

28) $\frac{26}{7}$ x $\frac{12}{5}$ = $\frac{312}{35}$ **or** $8\frac{32}{35}$

29) $\frac{3}{5}$ x $\frac{3}{2}$ = $\frac{9}{10}$

30) 3 x $\frac{2}{3}$ = **2**

1) $\frac{1}{6} \times \frac{5}{2} = \frac{5}{12}$

2) $\frac{39}{8} \times \frac{1}{2} = \frac{39}{16}$ **or** $2\frac{7}{16}$

3) $\frac{19}{8} \times \frac{10}{3} = \frac{95}{12}$ **or** $7\frac{11}{12}$

4) $\frac{3}{2} \times 5 = \frac{15}{2}$ **or** $7\frac{1}{2}$

5) $\frac{10}{3} \times 3 = $ **10**

6) $\frac{7}{4} \times \frac{3}{2} = \frac{21}{8}$ **or** $2\frac{5}{8}$

7) $1 \times \frac{4}{3} = \frac{4}{3}$ **or** $1\frac{1}{3}$

8) $\frac{17}{7} \times \frac{7}{2} = \frac{17}{2}$ **or** $8\frac{1}{2}$

9) $\frac{5}{4} \times \frac{3}{2} = \frac{15}{8}$ **or** $1\frac{7}{8}$

10) $2 \times \frac{1}{3} = \frac{2}{3}$

11) $4 \times \frac{2}{5} = \frac{8}{5}$ **or** $1\frac{3}{5}$

12) $2 \times \frac{10}{3} = \frac{20}{3}$ **or** $6\frac{2}{3}$

13) $4 \times \frac{5}{3} = \frac{20}{3}$ **or** $6\frac{2}{3}$

14) $4 \times \frac{3}{2} = $ **6**

15) $3 \times \frac{1}{3} = $ **1**

12/62

16) $\frac{12}{5} \times 4 = \frac{48}{5}$ **or** $9\frac{3}{5}$

17) $\frac{4}{5} \times 1 = \frac{4}{5}$

18) $2 \times \frac{19}{5} = \frac{38}{5}$ **or** $7\frac{3}{5}$

19) $\frac{27}{7} \times \frac{19}{5} = \frac{513}{35}$ **or** $14\frac{23}{35}$

20) $3 \times \frac{5}{2} = \frac{15}{2}$ **or** $7\frac{1}{2}$

21) $\frac{29}{7} \times \frac{5}{2} = \frac{145}{14}$ **or** $10\frac{5}{14}$

22) $\frac{16}{5} \times 4 = \frac{64}{5}$ **or** $12\frac{4}{5}$

23) $\frac{26}{7} \times 1 = \frac{26}{7}$ **or** $3\frac{5}{7}$

24) $\frac{5}{2} \times 4 = $ **10**

25) $\frac{7}{8} \times 1 = \frac{7}{8}$

26) $\frac{6}{7} \times \frac{1}{3} = \frac{2}{7}$

27) $\frac{1}{7} \times \frac{13}{3} = \frac{13}{21}$

28) $\frac{11}{3} \times \frac{5}{2} = \frac{55}{6}$ **or** $9\frac{1}{6}$

29) $\frac{19}{7} \times \frac{9}{2} = \frac{171}{14}$ **or** $12\frac{3}{14}$

30) $\frac{11}{5} \times \frac{3}{4} = \frac{33}{20}$ **or** $1\frac{13}{20}$

1) $\frac{21}{8} \times \frac{18}{5} = \frac{189}{20}$ **or** $9\frac{9}{20}$

2) $\frac{18}{7} \times 3 = \frac{54}{7}$ **or** $7\frac{5}{7}$

3) $\frac{1}{2} \times \frac{7}{2} = \frac{7}{4}$ **or** $1\frac{3}{4}$

4) $\frac{32}{7} \times 2 = \frac{64}{7}$ **or** $9\frac{1}{7}$

5) $\frac{23}{6} \times \frac{7}{2} = \frac{161}{12}$ **or** $13\frac{5}{12}$

6) $\frac{18}{5} \times 3 = \frac{54}{5}$ **or** $10\frac{4}{5}$

7) $\frac{13}{3} \times \frac{15}{4} = \frac{65}{4}$ **or** $16\frac{1}{4}$

8) $1 \times \frac{3}{2} = \frac{3}{2}$ **or** $1\frac{1}{2}$

9) $\frac{17}{6} \times \frac{1}{2} = \frac{17}{12}$ **or** $1\frac{5}{12}$

10) $\frac{33}{7} \times \frac{18}{5} = \frac{594}{35}$ **or** $16\frac{34}{35}$

11) $\frac{4}{3} \times \frac{17}{4} = \frac{17}{3}$ **or** $5\frac{2}{3}$

12) $3 \times \frac{12}{5} = \frac{36}{5}$ **or** $7\frac{1}{5}$

13) $\frac{8}{5} \times 2 = \frac{16}{5}$ **or** $3\frac{1}{5}$

14) $\frac{11}{4} \times \frac{10}{3} = \frac{55}{6}$ **or** $9\frac{1}{6}$

15) $\frac{8}{7} \times \frac{6}{5} = \frac{48}{35}$ **or** $1\frac{13}{35}$

13/62

16) $\frac{5}{4} \times \frac{1}{4} = \frac{5}{16}$

17) $\frac{21}{5} \times 1 = \frac{21}{5}$ **or** $4\frac{1}{5}$

18) $\frac{11}{8} \times 1 = \frac{11}{8}$ **or** $1\frac{3}{8}$

19) $3 \times \frac{15}{4} = \frac{45}{4}$ **or** $11\frac{1}{4}$

20) $\frac{17}{5} \times \frac{17}{4} = \frac{289}{20}$ **or** $14\frac{9}{20}$

21) $1 \times \frac{7}{3} = \frac{7}{3}$ **or** $2\frac{1}{3}$

22) $\frac{9}{2} \times 2 = $ **9**

23) $\frac{17}{4} \times \frac{5}{4} = \frac{85}{16}$ **or** $5\frac{5}{16}$

24) $\frac{7}{2} \times 1 = \frac{7}{2}$ **or** $3\frac{1}{2}$

25) $\frac{11}{4} \times \frac{16}{5} = \frac{44}{5}$ **or** $8\frac{4}{5}$

26) $\frac{3}{2} \times \frac{9}{2} = \frac{27}{4}$ **or** $6\frac{3}{4}$

27) $\frac{7}{3} \times 3 = $ **7**

28) $\frac{23}{5} \times \frac{5}{3} = \frac{23}{3}$ **or** $7\frac{2}{3}$

29) $\frac{3}{2} \times \frac{13}{5} = \frac{39}{10}$ **or** $3\frac{9}{10}$

30) $\frac{9}{4} \times 5 = \frac{45}{4}$ **or** $11\frac{1}{4}$

1) $\frac{1}{8}$ x 1 = $\frac{1}{8}$

2) $\frac{4}{5}$ x $\frac{13}{4}$ = $\frac{13}{5}$ **or** $2\frac{3}{5}$

3) $\frac{19}{8}$ x 3 = $\frac{57}{8}$ **or** $7\frac{1}{8}$

4) $\frac{1}{4}$ x $\frac{5}{2}$ = $\frac{5}{8}$

5) $\frac{6}{5}$ x $\frac{8}{5}$ = $\frac{48}{25}$ **or** $1\frac{23}{25}$

6) $\frac{7}{6}$ x 3 = $\frac{7}{2}$ **or** $3\frac{1}{2}$

7) 2 x $\frac{11}{3}$ = $\frac{22}{3}$ **or** $7\frac{1}{3}$

8) $\frac{1}{5}$ x $\frac{19}{4}$ = $\frac{19}{20}$

9) $\frac{5}{2}$ x 1 = $\frac{5}{2}$ **or** $2\frac{1}{2}$

10) $\frac{19}{4}$ x 2 = $\frac{19}{2}$ **or** $9\frac{1}{2}$

11) $\frac{19}{10}$ x $\frac{5}{2}$ = $\frac{19}{4}$ **or** $4\frac{3}{4}$

12) $\frac{8}{3}$ x $\frac{10}{3}$ = $\frac{80}{9}$ **or** $8\frac{8}{9}$

13) $\frac{13}{4}$ x 4 = **13**

14) $\frac{5}{9}$ x $\frac{3}{4}$ = $\frac{5}{12}$

15) $\frac{3}{5}$ x $\frac{5}{2}$ = $\frac{3}{2}$ **or** $1\frac{1}{2}$

14/62

16) $\frac{18}{5}$ x 2 = $\frac{36}{5}$ **or** $7\frac{1}{5}$

17) 3 x $\frac{3}{2}$ = $\frac{9}{2}$ **or** $4\frac{1}{2}$

18) $\frac{8}{5}$ x $\frac{9}{2}$ = $\frac{36}{5}$ **or** $7\frac{1}{5}$

19) $\frac{15}{8}$ x 4 = $\frac{15}{2}$ **or** $7\frac{1}{2}$

20) $\frac{11}{5}$ x $\frac{7}{3}$ = $\frac{77}{15}$ **or** $5\frac{2}{15}$

21) $\frac{7}{8}$ x $\frac{3}{2}$ = $\frac{21}{16}$ **or** $1\frac{5}{16}$

22) 2 x $\frac{13}{4}$ = $\frac{13}{2}$ **or** $6\frac{1}{2}$

23) $\frac{13}{6}$ x $\frac{19}{5}$ = $\frac{247}{30}$ **or** $8\frac{7}{30}$

24) $\frac{3}{2}$ x $\frac{13}{4}$ = $\frac{39}{8}$ **or** $4\frac{7}{8}$

25) $\frac{7}{5}$ x $\frac{9}{4}$ = $\frac{63}{20}$ **or** $3\frac{3}{20}$

26) $\frac{15}{8}$ x 1 = $\frac{15}{8}$ **or** $1\frac{7}{8}$

27) $\frac{7}{3}$ x 5 = $\frac{35}{3}$ **or** $11\frac{2}{3}$

28) $\frac{11}{6}$ x 3 = $\frac{11}{2}$ **or** $5\frac{1}{2}$

29) $\frac{7}{2}$ x $\frac{16}{5}$ = $\frac{56}{5}$ **or** $11\frac{1}{5}$

30) $\frac{7}{2}$ x $\frac{7}{2}$ = $\frac{49}{4}$ **or** $12\frac{1}{4}$

1) $\frac{19}{5}$ x $\frac{14}{3}$ = $\frac{266}{15}$ **or** $17\frac{11}{15}$

2) $\frac{15}{8}$ x $\frac{3}{2}$ = $\frac{45}{16}$ **or** $2\frac{13}{16}$

3) $\frac{11}{3}$ x $\frac{1}{2}$ = $\frac{11}{6}$ **or** $1\frac{5}{6}$

4) $\frac{14}{5}$ x 2 = $\frac{28}{5}$ **or** $5\frac{3}{5}$

5) $\frac{1}{2}$ x $\frac{8}{3}$ = $\frac{4}{3}$ **or** $1\frac{1}{3}$

6) $\frac{5}{3}$ x $\frac{1}{3}$ = $\frac{5}{9}$

7) $\frac{41}{10}$ x 2 = $\frac{41}{5}$ **or** $8\frac{1}{5}$

8) $\frac{24}{7}$ x 5 = $\frac{120}{7}$ **or** $17\frac{1}{7}$

9) $\frac{16}{5}$ x $\frac{1}{5}$ = $\frac{16}{25}$

10) $\frac{5}{3}$ x $\frac{18}{5}$ = **6**

11) $\frac{5}{4}$ x $\frac{5}{2}$ = $\frac{25}{8}$ **or** $3\frac{1}{8}$

12) $\frac{2}{3}$ x $\frac{8}{3}$ = $\frac{16}{9}$ **or** $1\frac{7}{9}$

13) $\frac{22}{7}$ x $\frac{13}{3}$ = $\frac{286}{21}$ **or** $13\frac{13}{21}$

14) $\frac{10}{3}$ x $\frac{1}{5}$ = $\frac{2}{3}$

15) $\frac{7}{2}$ x $\frac{13}{3}$ = $\frac{91}{6}$ **or** $15\frac{1}{6}$

15/62

16) $\frac{14}{5}$ x $\frac{3}{2}$ = $\frac{21}{5}$ **or** $4\frac{1}{5}$

17) $\frac{7}{8}$ x $\frac{1}{5}$ = $\frac{7}{40}$

18) $\frac{11}{7}$ x $\frac{2}{3}$ = $\frac{22}{21}$ **or** $1\frac{1}{21}$

19) $\frac{4}{3}$ x $\frac{1}{2}$ = $\frac{2}{3}$

20) $\frac{31}{7}$ x $\frac{5}{4}$ = $\frac{155}{28}$ **or** $5\frac{15}{28}$

21) $\frac{7}{3}$ x $\frac{13}{4}$ = $\frac{91}{12}$ **or** $7\frac{7}{12}$

22) $\frac{13}{7}$ x $\frac{16}{5}$ = $\frac{208}{35}$ **or** $5\frac{33}{35}$

23) $\frac{29}{7}$ x $\frac{7}{2}$ = $\frac{29}{2}$ **or** $14\frac{1}{2}$

24) $\frac{15}{4}$ x 3 = $\frac{45}{4}$ **or** $11\frac{1}{4}$

25) $\frac{13}{4}$ x $\frac{14}{3}$ = $\frac{91}{6}$ **or** $15\frac{1}{6}$

26) $\frac{20}{9}$ x 4 = $\frac{80}{9}$ **or** $8\frac{8}{9}$

27) $\frac{3}{2}$ x $\frac{11}{4}$ = $\frac{33}{8}$ **or** $4\frac{1}{8}$

28) $\frac{5}{4}$ x $\frac{9}{2}$ = $\frac{45}{8}$ **or** $5\frac{5}{8}$

29) $\frac{2}{3}$ x 3 = **2**

30) $\frac{11}{5}$ x 2 = $\frac{22}{5}$ **or** $4\frac{2}{5}$

1) $3 \times \frac{7}{2} = \frac{21}{2}$ **or** $10\frac{1}{2}$

2) $\frac{2}{5} \times 2 = \frac{4}{5}$

3) $\frac{3}{2} \times \frac{5}{2} = \frac{15}{4}$ **or** $3\frac{3}{4}$

4) $5 \times \frac{3}{2} = \frac{15}{2}$ **or** $7\frac{1}{2}$

5) $\frac{1}{2} \times \frac{7}{3} = \frac{7}{6}$ **or** $1\frac{1}{6}$

6) $\frac{30}{7} \times 2 = \frac{60}{7}$ **or** $8\frac{4}{7}$

7) $\frac{16}{7} \times \frac{1}{2} = \frac{8}{7}$ **or** $1\frac{1}{7}$

8) $4 \times \frac{2}{3} = \frac{8}{3}$ **or** $2\frac{2}{3}$

9) $\frac{9}{8} \times 4 = \frac{9}{2}$ **or** $4\frac{1}{2}$

10) $\frac{8}{3} \times 4 = \frac{32}{3}$ **or** $10\frac{2}{3}$

11) $\frac{8}{3} \times \frac{19}{5} = \frac{152}{15}$ **or** $10\frac{2}{15}$

12) $3 \times \frac{12}{5} = \frac{36}{5}$ **or** $7\frac{1}{5}$

13) $4 \times \frac{1}{2} = $ **2**

14) $\frac{24}{5} \times 3 = \frac{72}{5}$ **or** $14\frac{2}{5}$

15) $\frac{22}{5} \times \frac{9}{5} = \frac{198}{25}$ **or** $7\frac{23}{25}$

16/62

16) $3 \times \frac{11}{4} = \frac{33}{4}$ **or** $8\frac{1}{4}$

17) $\frac{35}{9} \times 1 = \frac{35}{9}$ **or** $3\frac{8}{9}$

18) $\frac{15}{4} \times \frac{1}{2} = \frac{15}{8}$ **or** $1\frac{7}{8}$

19) $\frac{16}{7} \times \frac{22}{5} = \frac{352}{35}$ **or** $10\frac{2}{35}$

20) $3 \times \frac{17}{4} = \frac{51}{4}$ **or** $12\frac{3}{4}$

21) $\frac{7}{2} \times \frac{5}{3} = \frac{35}{6}$ **or** $5\frac{5}{6}$

22) $\frac{9}{10} \times 2 = \frac{9}{5}$ **or** $1\frac{4}{5}$

23) $\frac{5}{2} \times \frac{1}{2} = \frac{5}{4}$ **or** $1\frac{1}{4}$

24) $\frac{3}{2} \times \frac{9}{2} = \frac{27}{4}$ **or** $6\frac{3}{4}$

25) $\frac{5}{3} \times 4 = \frac{20}{3}$ **or** $6\frac{2}{3}$

26) $\frac{33}{7} \times \frac{5}{2} = \frac{165}{14}$ **or** $11\frac{11}{14}$

27) $\frac{17}{4} \times 5 = \frac{85}{4}$ **or** $21\frac{1}{4}$

28) $\frac{35}{8} \times \frac{10}{3} = \frac{175}{12}$ **or** $14\frac{7}{12}$

29) $\frac{39}{8} \times 3 = \frac{117}{8}$ **or** $14\frac{5}{8}$

30) $\frac{22}{5} \times \frac{18}{5} = \frac{396}{25}$ **or** $15\frac{21}{25}$

1) $\frac{25}{8}$ x $\frac{16}{5}$ = **10**

2) $\frac{10}{7}$ x $\frac{14}{3}$ = $\frac{20}{3}$ **or** $6\frac{2}{3}$

3) $\frac{8}{9}$ x $\frac{19}{5}$ = $\frac{152}{45}$ **or** $3\frac{17}{45}$

4) 4 x $\frac{11}{4}$ = **11**

5) $\frac{21}{5}$ x 3 = $\frac{63}{5}$ **or** $12\frac{3}{5}$

6) $\frac{17}{5}$ x $\frac{7}{2}$ = $\frac{119}{10}$ **or** $11\frac{9}{10}$

7) $\frac{19}{4}$ x 3 = $\frac{57}{4}$ **or** $14\frac{1}{4}$

8) $\frac{1}{3}$ x 3 = **1**

9) 1 x $\frac{17}{4}$ = $\frac{17}{4}$ **or** $4\frac{1}{4}$

10) $\frac{24}{5}$ x $\frac{1}{5}$ = $\frac{24}{25}$

11) $\frac{5}{3}$ x 2 = $\frac{10}{3}$ **or** $3\frac{1}{3}$

12) 3 x $\frac{1}{2}$ = $\frac{3}{2}$ **or** $1\frac{1}{2}$

13) $\frac{30}{7}$ x $\frac{14}{5}$ = **12**

14) $\frac{19}{4}$ x $\frac{5}{2}$ = $\frac{95}{8}$ **or** $11\frac{7}{8}$

15) 2 x $\frac{17}{4}$ = $\frac{17}{2}$ **or** $8\frac{1}{2}$

17/62

16) $\frac{16}{9}$ x $\frac{9}{2}$ = **8**

17) $\frac{12}{5}$ x $\frac{5}{3}$ = **4**

18) $\frac{8}{3}$ x 3 = **8**

19) 4 x $\frac{3}{2}$ = **6**

20) $\frac{21}{5}$ x $\frac{9}{2}$ = $\frac{189}{10}$ **or** $18\frac{9}{10}$

21) $\frac{11}{3}$ x $\frac{9}{5}$ = $\frac{33}{5}$ **or** $6\frac{3}{5}$

22) $\frac{35}{8}$ x $\frac{1}{3}$ = $\frac{35}{24}$ **or** $1\frac{11}{24}$

23) $\frac{9}{2}$ x $\frac{1}{3}$ = $\frac{3}{2}$ **or** $1\frac{1}{2}$

24) $\frac{1}{9}$ x 2 = $\frac{2}{9}$

25) $\frac{1}{6}$ x 4 = $\frac{2}{3}$

26) $\frac{1}{2}$ x $\frac{1}{2}$ = $\frac{1}{4}$

27) $\frac{4}{5}$ x $\frac{5}{3}$ = $\frac{4}{3}$ **or** $1\frac{1}{3}$

28) $\frac{9}{2}$ x 3 = $\frac{27}{2}$ **or** $13\frac{1}{2}$

29) $\frac{27}{8}$ x $\frac{7}{2}$ = $\frac{189}{16}$ **or** $11\frac{13}{16}$

30) $\frac{3}{5}$ x 5 = **3**

1) $\frac{7}{10}$ x $\frac{7}{2}$ = $\frac{49}{20}$ **or** $2\frac{9}{20}$

2) $\frac{11}{3}$ x $\frac{7}{3}$ = $\frac{77}{9}$ **or** $8\frac{5}{9}$

3) $\frac{19}{4}$ x $\frac{13}{3}$ = $\frac{247}{12}$ **or** $20\frac{7}{12}$

4) $\frac{10}{9}$ x 1 = $\frac{10}{9}$ **or** $1\frac{1}{9}$

5) $\frac{22}{5}$ x $\frac{14}{5}$ = $\frac{308}{25}$ **or** $12\frac{8}{25}$

6) $\frac{3}{2}$ x $\frac{9}{2}$ = $\frac{27}{4}$ **or** $6\frac{3}{4}$

7) $\frac{1}{3}$ x $\frac{18}{5}$ = $\frac{6}{5}$ **or** $1\frac{1}{5}$

8) $\frac{19}{10}$ x $\frac{13}{3}$ = $\frac{247}{30}$ **or** $8\frac{7}{30}$

9) $\frac{15}{4}$ x $\frac{4}{3}$ = **5**

10) $\frac{32}{9}$ x $\frac{2}{3}$ = $\frac{64}{27}$ **or** $2\frac{10}{27}$

11) $\frac{4}{3}$ x 3 = **4**

12) 1 x $\frac{19}{5}$ = $\frac{19}{5}$ **or** $3\frac{4}{5}$

13) $\frac{38}{9}$ x 1 = $\frac{38}{9}$ **or** $4\frac{2}{9}$

14) $\frac{11}{9}$ x 4 = $\frac{44}{9}$ **or** $4\frac{8}{9}$

15) $\frac{3}{2}$ x $\frac{5}{2}$ = $\frac{15}{4}$ **or** $3\frac{3}{4}$

18/62

16) $\frac{11}{4}$ x 1 = $\frac{11}{4}$ **or** $2\frac{3}{4}$

17) 4 x $\frac{4}{3}$ = $\frac{16}{3}$ **or** $5\frac{1}{3}$

18) 1 x $\frac{14}{3}$ = $\frac{14}{3}$ **or** $4\frac{2}{3}$

19) $\frac{4}{9}$ x $\frac{3}{2}$ = $\frac{2}{3}$

20) $\frac{3}{2}$ x $\frac{10}{3}$ = **5**

21) 5 x $\frac{10}{3}$ = $\frac{50}{3}$ **or** $16\frac{2}{3}$

22) 1 x $\frac{4}{3}$ = $\frac{4}{3}$ **or** $1\frac{1}{3}$

23) $\frac{2}{5}$ x $\frac{22}{5}$ = $\frac{44}{25}$ **or** $1\frac{19}{25}$

24) 1 x $\frac{5}{2}$ = $\frac{5}{2}$ **or** $2\frac{1}{2}$

25) $\frac{5}{4}$ x $\frac{9}{2}$ = $\frac{45}{8}$ **or** $5\frac{5}{8}$

26) $\frac{4}{5}$ x 3 = $\frac{12}{5}$ **or** $2\frac{2}{5}$

27) $\frac{15}{4}$ x 5 = $\frac{75}{4}$ **or** $18\frac{3}{4}$

28) $\frac{10}{3}$ x $\frac{22}{5}$ = $\frac{44}{3}$ **or** $14\frac{2}{3}$

29) $\frac{11}{9}$ x $\frac{21}{5}$ = $\frac{77}{15}$ **or** $5\frac{2}{15}$

30) $\frac{19}{4}$ x 2 = $\frac{19}{2}$ **or** $9\frac{1}{2}$

1) $2 \times \frac{5}{4} = \frac{5}{2}$ **or** $2\frac{1}{2}$

2) $\frac{5}{3} \times \frac{17}{5} = \frac{17}{3}$ **or** $5\frac{2}{3}$

3) $\frac{13}{4} \times \frac{13}{4} = \frac{169}{16}$ **or** $10\frac{9}{16}$

4) $\frac{18}{7} \times \frac{2}{3} = \frac{12}{7}$ **or** $1\frac{5}{7}$

5) $\frac{1}{6} \times \frac{6}{5} = \frac{1}{5}$

6) $\frac{5}{2} \times \frac{3}{5} = \frac{3}{2}$ **or** $1\frac{1}{2}$

7) $\frac{6}{5} \times \frac{10}{3} = \mathbf{4}$

8) $\frac{10}{3} \times \frac{1}{2} = \frac{5}{3}$ **or** $1\frac{2}{3}$

9) $\frac{5}{3} \times \frac{3}{2} = \frac{5}{2}$ **or** $2\frac{1}{2}$

10) $\frac{6}{7} \times 2 = \frac{12}{7}$ **or** $1\frac{5}{7}$

11) $1 \times \frac{13}{5} = \frac{13}{5}$ **or** $2\frac{3}{5}$

12) $\frac{13}{5} \times \frac{11}{3} = \frac{143}{15}$ **or** $9\frac{8}{15}$

13) $\frac{18}{5} \times \frac{19}{4} = \frac{171}{10}$ **or** $17\frac{1}{10}$

14) $\frac{11}{8} \times \frac{11}{4} = \frac{121}{32}$ **or** $3\frac{25}{32}$

15) $\frac{29}{7} \times \frac{7}{2} = \frac{29}{2}$ **or** $14\frac{1}{2}$

19/62

16) $\frac{6}{7} \times \frac{9}{4} = \frac{27}{14}$ **or** $1\frac{13}{14}$

17) $1 \times \frac{17}{4} = \frac{17}{4}$ **or** $4\frac{1}{4}$

18) $\frac{23}{5} \times 1 = \frac{23}{5}$ **or** $4\frac{3}{5}$

19) $\frac{7}{3} \times \frac{9}{2} = \frac{21}{2}$ **or** $10\frac{1}{2}$

20) $\frac{35}{9} \times \frac{1}{2} = \frac{35}{18}$ **or** $1\frac{17}{18}$

21) $\frac{1}{6} \times \frac{22}{5} = \frac{11}{15}$

22) $\frac{4}{7} \times \frac{3}{4} = \frac{3}{7}$

23) $\frac{2}{5} \times 1 = \frac{2}{5}$

24) $\frac{9}{4} \times \frac{11}{3} = \frac{33}{4}$ **or** $8\frac{1}{4}$

25) $\frac{11}{3} \times 4 = \frac{44}{3}$ **or** $14\frac{2}{3}$

26) $\frac{13}{3} \times \frac{1}{2} = \frac{13}{6}$ **or** $2\frac{1}{6}$

27) $\frac{1}{2} \times \frac{12}{5} = \frac{6}{5}$ **or** $1\frac{1}{5}$

28) $5 \times \frac{1}{4} = \frac{5}{4}$ **or** $1\frac{1}{4}$

29) $\frac{10}{7} \times \frac{7}{2} = \mathbf{5}$

30) $\frac{7}{8} \times \frac{5}{3} = \frac{35}{24}$ **or** $1\frac{11}{24}$

1) $\frac{27}{8} \times 1 = \frac{27}{8}$ **or** $3\frac{3}{8}$

2) $\frac{9}{2} \times \frac{21}{5} = \frac{189}{10}$ **or** $18\frac{9}{10}$

3) $\frac{31}{9} \times \frac{7}{5} = \frac{217}{45}$ **or** $4\frac{37}{45}$

4) $\frac{9}{2} \times \frac{6}{5} = \frac{27}{5}$ **or** $5\frac{2}{5}$

5) $\frac{8}{3} \times \frac{9}{2} = $ **12**

6) $4 \times \frac{19}{4} = $ **19**

7) $\frac{7}{10} \times \frac{10}{3} = \frac{7}{3}$ **or** $2\frac{1}{3}$

8) $\frac{29}{10} \times \frac{5}{2} = \frac{29}{4}$ **or** $7\frac{1}{4}$

9) $\frac{39}{10} \times \frac{11}{3} = \frac{143}{10}$ **or** $14\frac{3}{10}$

10) $\frac{1}{5} \times \frac{3}{2} = \frac{3}{10}$

11) $4 \times \frac{11}{3} = \frac{44}{3}$ **or** $14\frac{2}{3}$

12) $\frac{32}{7} \times \frac{7}{2} = $ **16**

13) $\frac{1}{5} \times \frac{9}{2} = \frac{9}{10}$

14) $\frac{7}{10} \times \frac{7}{2} = \frac{49}{20}$ **or** $2\frac{9}{20}$

15) $3 \times \frac{7}{4} = \frac{21}{4}$ **or** $5\frac{1}{4}$

20/62

16) $\frac{3}{2} \times 3 = \frac{9}{2}$ **or** $4\frac{1}{2}$

17) $\frac{22}{5} \times \frac{4}{3} = \frac{88}{15}$ **or** $5\frac{13}{15}$

18) $\frac{19}{6} \times \frac{9}{4} = \frac{57}{8}$ **or** $7\frac{1}{8}$

19) $\frac{30}{7} \times \frac{5}{2} = \frac{75}{7}$ **or** $10\frac{5}{7}$

20) $\frac{37}{10} \times \frac{13}{3} = \frac{481}{30}$ **or** $16\frac{1}{30}$

21) $\frac{4}{3} \times 3 = $ **4**

22) $\frac{7}{2} \times \frac{5}{4} = \frac{35}{8}$ **or** $4\frac{3}{8}$

23) $\frac{7}{6} \times \frac{19}{5} = \frac{133}{30}$ **or** $4\frac{13}{30}$

24) $4 \times \frac{1}{2} = $ **2**

25) $\frac{23}{9} \times 3 = \frac{23}{3}$ **or** $7\frac{2}{3}$

26) $\frac{7}{2} \times \frac{5}{4} = \frac{35}{8}$ **or** $4\frac{3}{8}$

27) $\frac{5}{2} \times 5 = \frac{25}{2}$ **or** $12\frac{1}{2}$

28) $\frac{9}{4} \times \frac{5}{2} = \frac{45}{8}$ **or** $5\frac{5}{8}$

29) $\frac{9}{2} \times \frac{4}{3} = $ **6**

30) $\frac{7}{3} \times 4 = \frac{28}{3}$ **or** $9\frac{1}{3}$

1) $\frac{2}{5} \div \frac{1}{5} =$ **2**

2) $\frac{1}{2} \div \frac{1}{2} =$ **1**

3) $\frac{2}{5} \div \frac{5}{7} = \frac{14}{25}$

4) $\frac{3}{5} \div \frac{1}{2} = \frac{6}{5}$ **or** $1\frac{1}{5}$

5) $\frac{2}{3} \div \frac{3}{4} = \frac{8}{9}$

6) $\frac{1}{2} \div \frac{1}{2} =$ **1**

7) $\frac{3}{4} \div \frac{1}{3} = \frac{9}{4}$ **or** $2\frac{1}{4}$

8) $\frac{1}{3} \div \frac{1}{7} = \frac{7}{3}$ **or** $2\frac{1}{3}$

9) $\frac{1}{2} \div \frac{6}{7} = \frac{7}{12}$

10) $\frac{1}{2} \div 1 = \frac{1}{2}$

11) $\frac{3}{4} \div \frac{2}{5} = \frac{15}{8}$ **or** $1\frac{7}{8}$

12) $\frac{4}{5} \div \frac{3}{7} = \frac{28}{15}$ **or** $1\frac{13}{15}$

13) $\frac{1}{4} \div \frac{1}{2} = \frac{1}{2}$

14) $\frac{1}{2} \div \frac{1}{2} =$ **1**

15) $\frac{1}{3} \div \frac{5}{7} = \frac{7}{15}$

16) $\frac{1}{3} \div \frac{4}{5} = \frac{5}{12}$

17) $\frac{1}{2} \div \frac{3}{5} = \frac{5}{6}$

18) $\frac{1}{3} \div \frac{1}{2} = \frac{2}{3}$

19) $\frac{1}{2} \div \frac{4}{7} = \frac{7}{8}$

20) $\frac{4}{5} \div \frac{7}{8} = \frac{32}{35}$

21) $\frac{1}{2} \div \frac{4}{5} = \frac{5}{8}$

22) $\frac{1}{3} \div \frac{1}{3} =$ **1**

23) $\frac{3}{4} \div \frac{3}{8} =$ **2**

24) $\frac{1}{2} \div \frac{5}{8} = \frac{4}{5}$

25) $\frac{1}{2} \div \frac{1}{3} = \frac{3}{2}$ **or** $1\frac{1}{2}$

26) $\frac{4}{5} \div \frac{1}{4} = \frac{16}{5}$ **or** $3\frac{1}{5}$

27) $\frac{1}{2} \div \frac{1}{4} =$ **2**

28) $\frac{3}{5} \div \frac{4}{5} = \frac{3}{4}$

29) $\frac{1}{2} \div \frac{3}{5} = \frac{5}{6}$

30) $\frac{1}{2} \div \frac{6}{7} = \frac{7}{12}$

21/62

1) $\frac{2}{3} \div \frac{1}{2} = \frac{4}{3}$ **or** $1\frac{1}{3}$

2) $\frac{1}{2} \div \frac{1}{5} = \frac{5}{2}$ **or** $2\frac{1}{2}$

3) $\frac{1}{2} \div \frac{7}{8} = \frac{4}{7}$

4) $\frac{2}{3} \div \frac{5}{8} = \frac{16}{15}$ **or** $1\frac{1}{15}$

5) $\frac{1}{2} \div \frac{3}{5} = \frac{5}{6}$

6) $1 \div \frac{7}{8} = \frac{8}{7}$ **or** $1\frac{1}{7}$

7) $\frac{3}{4} \div \frac{1}{7} = \frac{21}{4}$ **or** $5\frac{1}{4}$

8) $\frac{3}{4} \div \frac{3}{8} = $ **2**

9) $\frac{1}{2} \div \frac{6}{7} = \frac{7}{12}$

10) $\frac{2}{5} \div \frac{1}{7} = \frac{14}{5}$ **or** $2\frac{4}{5}$

11) $\frac{3}{5} \div \frac{1}{4} = \frac{12}{5}$ **or** $2\frac{2}{5}$

12) $\frac{1}{2} \div \frac{1}{2} = $ **1**

13) $\frac{3}{5} \div \frac{2}{3} = \frac{9}{10}$

14) $\frac{1}{2} \div \frac{1}{2} = $ **1**

15) $\frac{1}{5} \div \frac{4}{7} = \frac{7}{20}$

16) $\frac{1}{2} \div \frac{1}{4} = $ **2**

17) $\frac{1}{2} \div \frac{2}{3} = \frac{3}{4}$

18) $\frac{2}{3} \div \frac{1}{4} = \frac{8}{3}$ **or** $2\frac{2}{3}$

19) $\frac{1}{3} \div \frac{4}{7} = \frac{7}{12}$

20) $\frac{1}{2} \div \frac{1}{8} = $ **4**

21) $\frac{1}{4} \div \frac{3}{4} = \frac{1}{3}$

22) $\frac{1}{2} \div \frac{1}{2} = $ **1**

23) $\frac{3}{4} \div \frac{1}{2} = \frac{3}{2}$ **or** $1\frac{1}{2}$

24) $\frac{2}{3} \div \frac{4}{5} = \frac{5}{6}$

25) $\frac{1}{2} \div \frac{5}{7} = \frac{7}{10}$

26) $\frac{1}{2} \div \frac{1}{2} = $ **1**

27) $\frac{1}{2} \div \frac{7}{8} = \frac{4}{7}$

28) $\frac{1}{2} \div \frac{3}{8} = \frac{4}{3}$ **or** $1\frac{1}{3}$

29) $\frac{3}{4} \div \frac{1}{2} = \frac{3}{2}$ **or** $1\frac{1}{2}$

30) $\frac{2}{3} \div \frac{1}{2} = \frac{4}{3}$ **or** $1\frac{1}{3}$

22/62

1) $\frac{1}{3} \div \frac{2}{3} = \frac{1}{2}$

2) $\frac{1}{2} \div \frac{5}{7} = \frac{7}{10}$

3) $\frac{1}{5} \div \frac{1}{3} = \frac{3}{5}$

4) $\frac{1}{2} \div \frac{1}{2} =$ **1**

5) $\frac{2}{5} \div \frac{1}{2} = \frac{4}{5}$

6) $\frac{1}{2} \div \frac{5}{6} = \frac{3}{5}$

7) $\frac{3}{5} \div \frac{1}{7} = \frac{21}{5}$ **or** $4\frac{1}{5}$

8) $\frac{1}{3} \div \frac{3}{4} = \frac{4}{9}$

9) $\frac{1}{2} \div \frac{1}{4} =$ **2**

10) $\frac{3}{5} \div \frac{4}{7} = \frac{21}{20}$ **or** $1\frac{1}{20}$

11) $\frac{3}{5} \div \frac{1}{3} = \frac{9}{5}$ **or** $1\frac{4}{5}$

12) $\frac{3}{4} \div \frac{1}{2} = \frac{3}{2}$ **or** $1\frac{1}{2}$

13) $\frac{1}{3} \div \frac{1}{3} =$ **1**

14) $\frac{1}{2} \div \frac{6}{7} = \frac{7}{12}$

15) $\frac{2}{3} \div \frac{1}{4} = \frac{8}{3}$ **or** $2\frac{2}{3}$

16) $\frac{1}{2} \div \frac{1}{2} =$ **1**

17) $\frac{1}{2} \div \frac{5}{6} = \frac{3}{5}$

18) $\frac{1}{3} \div \frac{1}{7} = \frac{7}{3}$ **or** $2\frac{1}{3}$

19) $\frac{2}{3} \div \frac{1}{2} = \frac{4}{3}$ **or** $1\frac{1}{3}$

20) $\frac{1}{4} \div \frac{1}{3} = \frac{3}{4}$

21) $\frac{2}{3} \div \frac{5}{7} = \frac{14}{15}$

22) $\frac{2}{3} \div \frac{1}{3} =$ **2**

23) $1 \div \frac{1}{5} =$ **5**

24) $\frac{2}{5} \div \frac{1}{2} = \frac{4}{5}$

25) $\frac{1}{4} \div \frac{3}{8} = \frac{2}{3}$

26) $\frac{2}{3} \div \frac{3}{4} = \frac{8}{9}$

27) $\frac{3}{5} \div \frac{3}{5} =$ **1**

28) $\frac{1}{3} \div \frac{1}{2} = \frac{2}{3}$

29) $\frac{1}{2} \div \frac{5}{6} = \frac{3}{5}$

30) $\frac{1}{2} \div \frac{1}{2} =$ **1**

23/62

1) $\frac{1}{2} \div \frac{2}{5} = \frac{5}{4}$ **or** $1\frac{1}{4}$

2) $\frac{1}{4} \div \frac{3}{4} = \frac{1}{3}$

3) $\frac{1}{3} \div \frac{2}{3} = \frac{1}{2}$

4) $\frac{1}{2} \div \frac{5}{7} = \frac{7}{10}$

5) $\frac{2}{3} \div \frac{5}{7} = \frac{14}{15}$

6) $1 \div \frac{2}{3} = \frac{3}{2}$ **or** $1\frac{1}{2}$

7) $\frac{1}{5} \div \frac{1}{6} = \frac{6}{5}$ **or** $1\frac{1}{5}$

8) $\frac{1}{4} \div \frac{1}{2} = \frac{1}{2}$

9) $\frac{1}{2} \div \frac{1}{2} = $ **1**

10) $\frac{2}{3} \div \frac{1}{4} = \frac{8}{3}$ **or** $2\frac{2}{3}$

11) $\frac{2}{3} \div \frac{7}{8} = \frac{16}{21}$

12) $\frac{1}{5} \div \frac{1}{5} = $ **1**

13) $\frac{1}{2} \div \frac{5}{6} = \frac{3}{5}$

14) $\frac{3}{4} \div \frac{3}{4} = $ **1**

15) $\frac{3}{5} \div \frac{2}{5} = \frac{3}{2}$ **or** $1\frac{1}{2}$

16) $\frac{1}{5} \div \frac{1}{3} = \frac{3}{5}$

17) $\frac{1}{2} \div \frac{3}{7} = \frac{7}{6}$ **or** $1\frac{1}{6}$

18) $\frac{3}{4} \div \frac{3}{4} = $ **1**

19) $\frac{1}{2} \div \frac{1}{2} = $ **1**

20) $\frac{2}{5} \div \frac{3}{4} = \frac{8}{15}$

21) $\frac{1}{5} \div \frac{1}{2} = \frac{2}{5}$

22) $\frac{4}{5} \div \frac{5}{7} = \frac{28}{25}$ **or** $1\frac{3}{25}$

23) $\frac{3}{4} \div \frac{1}{7} = \frac{21}{4}$ **or** $5\frac{1}{4}$

24) $\frac{3}{5} \div \frac{4}{5} = \frac{3}{4}$

25) $\frac{1}{3} \div \frac{1}{2} = \frac{2}{3}$

26) $\frac{1}{2} \div \frac{6}{7} = \frac{7}{12}$

27) $\frac{1}{2} \div \frac{1}{7} = \frac{7}{2}$ **or** $3\frac{1}{2}$

28) $\frac{3}{4} \div \frac{3}{8} = $ **2**

29) $\frac{1}{2} \div \frac{1}{7} = \frac{7}{2}$ **or** $3\frac{1}{2}$

30) $\frac{3}{4} \div \frac{4}{7} = \frac{21}{16}$ **or** $1\frac{5}{16}$

24/62

1) $\frac{1}{2} \div \frac{1}{2} =$ **1**

2) $\frac{1}{2} \div \frac{7}{8} = \frac{4}{7}$

3) $\frac{4}{5} \div \frac{2}{5} =$ **2**

4) $\frac{1}{2} \div \frac{4}{5} = \frac{5}{8}$

5) $\frac{3}{4} \div \frac{1}{2} = \frac{3}{2}$ **or** $1\frac{1}{2}$

6) $\frac{2}{3} \div \frac{5}{7} = \frac{14}{15}$

7) $\frac{3}{5} \div \frac{2}{3} = \frac{9}{10}$

8) $\frac{1}{4} \div \frac{1}{2} = \frac{1}{2}$

9) $\frac{1}{2} \div \frac{1}{3} = \frac{3}{2}$ **or** $1\frac{1}{2}$

10) $\frac{2}{3} \div \frac{1}{8} = \frac{16}{3}$ **or** $5\frac{1}{3}$

11) $\frac{1}{2} \div \frac{1}{4} =$ **2**

12) $\frac{1}{2} \div \frac{3}{4} = \frac{2}{3}$

13) $\frac{1}{2} \div \frac{2}{3} = \frac{3}{4}$

14) $\frac{4}{5} \div \frac{1}{3} = \frac{12}{5}$ **or** $2\frac{2}{5}$

15) $\frac{2}{5} \div \frac{1}{7} = \frac{14}{5}$ **or** $2\frac{4}{5}$

16) $\frac{3}{4} \div \frac{2}{7} = \frac{21}{8}$ **or** $2\frac{5}{8}$

17) $\frac{1}{5} \div \frac{3}{4} = \frac{4}{15}$

18) $\frac{3}{4} \div \frac{1}{2} = \frac{3}{2}$ **or** $1\frac{1}{2}$

19) $\frac{1}{2} \div \frac{2}{7} = \frac{7}{4}$ **or** $1\frac{3}{4}$

20) $\frac{4}{5} \div \frac{2}{3} = \frac{6}{5}$ **or** $1\frac{1}{5}$

21) $\frac{1}{3} \div \frac{1}{2} = \frac{2}{3}$

22) $\frac{1}{3} \div \frac{3}{4} = \frac{4}{9}$

23) $\frac{1}{5} \div \frac{1}{2} = \frac{2}{5}$

24) $\frac{1}{4} \div \frac{2}{3} = \frac{3}{8}$

25) $\frac{1}{2} \div \frac{2}{5} = \frac{5}{4}$ **or** $1\frac{1}{4}$

26) $\frac{1}{3} \div \frac{5}{6} = \frac{2}{5}$

27) $1 \div \frac{1}{7} =$ **7**

28) $\frac{1}{2} \div \frac{1}{2} =$ **1**

29) $\frac{4}{5} \div \frac{2}{3} = \frac{6}{5}$ **or** $1\frac{1}{5}$

30) $\frac{3}{5} \div \frac{2}{5} = \frac{3}{2}$ **or** $1\frac{1}{2}$

25/62

1) $\frac{1}{2} \div \frac{3}{4} = \frac{2}{3}$

2) $\frac{3}{4} \div \frac{2}{3} = \frac{9}{8}$ **or** $1\frac{1}{8}$

3) $\frac{1}{4} \div \frac{1}{2} = \frac{1}{2}$

4) $\frac{1}{2} \div \frac{5}{6} = \frac{3}{5}$

5) $\frac{3}{4} \div \frac{7}{8} = \frac{6}{7}$

6) $\frac{1}{4} \div \frac{1}{3} = \frac{3}{4}$

7) $\frac{1}{3} \div \frac{2}{5} = \frac{5}{6}$

8) $\frac{2}{5} \div \frac{1}{2} = \frac{4}{5}$

9) $\frac{1}{5} \div \frac{1}{2} = \frac{2}{5}$

10) $\frac{1}{4} \div \frac{1}{2} = \frac{1}{2}$

11) $\frac{4}{5} \div \frac{2}{3} = \frac{6}{5}$ **or** $1\frac{1}{5}$

12) $\frac{1}{2} \div \frac{2}{3} = \frac{3}{4}$

13) $\frac{1}{2} \div \frac{1}{6} = $ **3**

14) $\frac{1}{3} \div \frac{3}{7} = \frac{7}{9}$

15) $\frac{1}{2} \div \frac{1}{3} = \frac{3}{2}$ **or** $1\frac{1}{2}$

26/62

16) $\frac{2}{3} \div \frac{3}{4} = \frac{8}{9}$

17) $\frac{3}{4} \div \frac{3}{4} = $ **1**

18) $\frac{2}{3} \div \frac{3}{7} = \frac{14}{9}$ **or** $1\frac{5}{9}$

19) $\frac{1}{2} \div \frac{1}{2} = $ **1**

20) $\frac{1}{2} \div \frac{3}{7} = \frac{7}{6}$ **or** $1\frac{1}{6}$

21) $\frac{1}{2} \div \frac{1}{4} = $ **2**

22) $\frac{2}{3} \div \frac{1}{2} = \frac{4}{3}$ **or** $1\frac{1}{3}$

23) $\frac{1}{2} \div \frac{3}{8} = \frac{4}{3}$ **or** $1\frac{1}{3}$

24) $\frac{1}{2} \div \frac{7}{8} = \frac{4}{7}$

25) $\frac{1}{4} \div \frac{2}{5} = \frac{5}{8}$

26) $\frac{2}{3} \div \frac{2}{3} = $ **1**

27) $\frac{4}{5} \div 1 = \frac{4}{5}$

28) $\frac{1}{2} \div \frac{2}{5} = \frac{5}{4}$ **or** $1\frac{1}{4}$

29) $\frac{2}{5} \div \frac{3}{8} = \frac{16}{15}$ **or** $1\frac{1}{15}$

30) $\frac{3}{4} \div \frac{1}{3} = \frac{9}{4}$ **or** $2\frac{1}{4}$

1) $\frac{1}{4} \div \frac{6}{7} = \frac{7}{24}$

2) $\frac{1}{2} \div \frac{1}{2} = $ **1**

3) $\frac{1}{3} \div \frac{1}{4} = \frac{4}{3}$ **or** $1\frac{1}{3}$

4) $\frac{3}{4} \div \frac{1}{5} = \frac{15}{4}$ **or** $3\frac{3}{4}$

5) $\frac{4}{5} \div \frac{2}{3} = \frac{6}{5}$ **or** $1\frac{1}{5}$

6) $\frac{1}{2} \div \frac{1}{3} = \frac{3}{2}$ **or** $1\frac{1}{2}$

7) $\frac{2}{5} \div \frac{1}{8} = \frac{16}{5}$ **or** $3\frac{1}{5}$

8) $\frac{1}{3} \div \frac{1}{3} = $ **1**

9) $\frac{2}{3} \div \frac{5}{6} = \frac{4}{5}$

10) $\frac{3}{4} \div \frac{4}{5} = \frac{15}{16}$

11) $\frac{1}{5} \div \frac{3}{8} = \frac{8}{15}$

12) $\frac{2}{3} \div \frac{3}{7} = \frac{14}{9}$ **or** $1\frac{5}{9}$

13) $\frac{4}{5} \div \frac{1}{2} = \frac{8}{5}$ **or** $1\frac{3}{5}$

14) $\frac{2}{3} \div \frac{1}{2} = \frac{4}{3}$ **or** $1\frac{1}{3}$

15) $\frac{1}{2} \div \frac{3}{4} = \frac{2}{3}$

27/62

16) $\frac{1}{4} \div \frac{3}{4} = \frac{1}{3}$

17) $\frac{1}{3} \div \frac{2}{5} = \frac{5}{6}$

18) $\frac{2}{3} \div \frac{2}{7} = \frac{7}{3}$ **or** $2\frac{1}{3}$

19) $\frac{1}{2} \div \frac{3}{4} = \frac{2}{3}$

20) $\frac{1}{2} \div \frac{1}{2} = $ **1**

21) $\frac{2}{3} \div \frac{2}{3} = $ **1**

22) $\frac{1}{3} \div \frac{4}{7} = \frac{7}{12}$

23) $\frac{1}{2} \div \frac{1}{8} = $ **4**

24) $\frac{2}{3} \div \frac{1}{3} = $ **2**

25) $\frac{1}{4} \div \frac{1}{4} = $ **1**

26) $\frac{1}{5} \div \frac{1}{4} = \frac{4}{5}$

27) $\frac{1}{5} \div \frac{4}{7} = \frac{7}{20}$

28) $1 \div \frac{3}{5} = \frac{5}{3}$ **or** $1\frac{2}{3}$

29) $\frac{4}{5} \div \frac{1}{3} = \frac{12}{5}$ **or** $2\frac{2}{5}$

30) $\frac{1}{2} \div \frac{1}{4} = $ **2**

1) $\frac{1}{2} \div \frac{3}{5} = \frac{5}{6}$

2) $\frac{1}{2} \div 1 = \frac{1}{2}$

3) $\frac{2}{5} \div \frac{2}{3} = \frac{3}{5}$

4) $\frac{2}{3} \div \frac{1}{4} = \frac{8}{3}$ **or** $2\frac{2}{3}$

5) $\frac{2}{3} \div \frac{4}{7} = \frac{7}{6}$ **or** $1\frac{1}{6}$

6) $\frac{3}{4} \div \frac{1}{2} = \frac{3}{2}$ **or** $1\frac{1}{2}$

7) $\frac{1}{2} \div \frac{1}{2} = \mathbf{1}$

8) $\frac{1}{5} \div \frac{1}{4} = \frac{4}{5}$

9) $\frac{2}{3} \div \frac{3}{8} = \frac{16}{9}$ **or** $1\frac{7}{9}$

10) $\frac{1}{2} \div \frac{7}{8} = \frac{4}{7}$

11) $\frac{1}{4} \div \frac{3}{4} = \frac{1}{3}$

12) $\frac{1}{2} \div \frac{1}{6} = \mathbf{3}$

13) $\frac{2}{5} \div \frac{4}{5} = \frac{1}{2}$

14) $\frac{2}{3} \div \frac{2}{7} = \frac{7}{3}$ **or** $2\frac{1}{3}$

15) $\frac{4}{5} \div \frac{4}{7} = \frac{7}{5}$ **or** $1\frac{2}{5}$

16) $\frac{3}{4} \div \frac{6}{7} = \frac{7}{8}$

17) $\frac{1}{2} \div \frac{1}{5} = \frac{5}{2}$ **or** $2\frac{1}{2}$

18) $\frac{3}{5} \div \frac{3}{4} = \frac{4}{5}$

19) $\frac{1}{3} \div \frac{1}{2} = \frac{2}{3}$

20) $\frac{1}{5} \div \frac{4}{7} = \frac{7}{20}$

21) $\frac{1}{3} \div \frac{4}{5} = \frac{5}{12}$

22) $\frac{2}{3} \div \frac{1}{4} = \frac{8}{3}$ **or** $2\frac{2}{3}$

23) $\frac{1}{2} \div \frac{1}{2} = \mathbf{1}$

24) $\frac{1}{2} \div \frac{2}{3} = \frac{3}{4}$

25) $\frac{1}{2} \div \frac{1}{6} = \mathbf{3}$

26) $\frac{2}{5} \div \frac{1}{2} = \frac{4}{5}$

27) $\frac{2}{3} \div \frac{5}{7} = \frac{14}{15}$

28) $\frac{2}{3} \div \frac{1}{2} = \frac{4}{3}$ **or** $1\frac{1}{3}$

29) $\frac{4}{5} \div \frac{1}{2} = \frac{8}{5}$ **or** $1\frac{3}{5}$

30) $\frac{2}{3} \div \frac{3}{4} = \frac{8}{9}$

28/62

1) $\frac{1}{2} \div \frac{1}{2} =$ **1**

2) $\frac{1}{3} \div \frac{1}{6} =$ **2**

3) $\frac{1}{2} \div \frac{1}{3} = \frac{3}{2}$ **or** $1\frac{1}{2}$

4) $\frac{2}{3} \div \frac{2}{3} =$ **1**

5) $\frac{1}{3} \div \frac{1}{2} = \frac{2}{3}$

6) $\frac{2}{5} \div \frac{1}{2} = \frac{4}{5}$

7) $\frac{1}{3} \div \frac{1}{2} = \frac{2}{3}$

8) $\frac{2}{3} \div \frac{1}{2} = \frac{4}{3}$ **or** $1\frac{1}{3}$

9) $\frac{1}{2} \div \frac{1}{2} =$ **1**

10) $\frac{4}{5} \div \frac{3}{5} = \frac{4}{3}$ **or** $1\frac{1}{3}$

11) $\frac{3}{5} \div \frac{5}{6} = \frac{18}{25}$

12) $\frac{1}{2} \div \frac{1}{7} = \frac{7}{2}$ **or** $3\frac{1}{2}$

13) $\frac{1}{3} \div \frac{3}{4} = \frac{4}{9}$

14) $\frac{1}{2} \div \frac{3}{8} = \frac{4}{3}$ **or** $1\frac{1}{3}$

15) $\frac{3}{5} \div \frac{3}{4} = \frac{4}{5}$

16) $\frac{1}{3} \div \frac{2}{3} = \frac{1}{2}$

17) $\frac{1}{5} \div \frac{2}{3} = \frac{3}{10}$

18) $\frac{1}{4} \div \frac{1}{7} = \frac{7}{4}$ **or** $1\frac{3}{4}$

19) $\frac{4}{5} \div \frac{1}{4} = \frac{16}{5}$ **or** $3\frac{1}{5}$

20) $\frac{1}{2} \div \frac{4}{5} = \frac{5}{8}$

21) $\frac{1}{2} \div \frac{1}{3} = \frac{3}{2}$ **or** $1\frac{1}{2}$

22) $\frac{4}{5} \div \frac{1}{2} = \frac{8}{5}$ **or** $1\frac{3}{5}$

23) $\frac{1}{2} \div \frac{4}{5} = \frac{5}{8}$

24) $\frac{1}{2} \div \frac{1}{2} =$ **1**

25) $\frac{3}{5} \div \frac{2}{3} = \frac{9}{10}$

26) $\frac{3}{4} \div \frac{2}{3} = \frac{9}{8}$ **or** $1\frac{1}{8}$

27) $\frac{2}{5} \div \frac{3}{4} = \frac{8}{15}$

28) $\frac{1}{2} \div \frac{3}{8} = \frac{4}{3}$ **or** $1\frac{1}{3}$

29) $\frac{1}{2} \div \frac{2}{3} = \frac{3}{4}$

30) $\frac{1}{4} \div \frac{1}{2} = \frac{1}{2}$

29/62

1) $\frac{3}{5} \div \frac{2}{5} = \frac{3}{2}$ **or** $1\frac{1}{2}$

2) $\frac{1}{3} \div \frac{3}{8} = \frac{8}{9}$

3) $\frac{1}{3} \div \frac{7}{8} = \frac{8}{21}$

4) $\frac{3}{5} \div \frac{1}{5} = $ **3**

5) $\frac{1}{2} \div \frac{1}{3} = \frac{3}{2}$ **or** $1\frac{1}{2}$

6) $\frac{1}{2} \div \frac{2}{3} = \frac{3}{4}$

7) $\frac{1}{5} \div \frac{2}{3} = \frac{3}{10}$

8) $\frac{1}{2} \div \frac{1}{2} = $ **1**

9) $\frac{2}{5} \div \frac{5}{7} = \frac{14}{25}$

10) $\frac{3}{4} \div \frac{1}{5} = \frac{15}{4}$ **or** $3\frac{3}{4}$

11) $\frac{1}{4} \div \frac{1}{2} = \frac{1}{2}$

12) $\frac{1}{2} \div \frac{1}{5} = \frac{5}{2}$ **or** $2\frac{1}{2}$

13) $\frac{1}{2} \div \frac{3}{7} = \frac{7}{6}$ **or** $1\frac{1}{6}$

14) $\frac{1}{3} \div \frac{1}{2} = \frac{2}{3}$

15) $\frac{2}{3} \div \frac{1}{2} = \frac{4}{3}$ **or** $1\frac{1}{3}$

16) $\frac{2}{3} \div \frac{2}{3} = $ **1**

17) $\frac{3}{4} \div \frac{2}{5} = \frac{15}{8}$ **or** $1\frac{7}{8}$

18) $\frac{2}{5} \div \frac{1}{2} = \frac{4}{5}$

19) $\frac{1}{2} \div \frac{2}{3} = \frac{3}{4}$

20) $\frac{1}{2} \div \frac{1}{4} = $ **2**

21) $\frac{2}{5} \div \frac{5}{6} = \frac{12}{25}$

22) $\frac{2}{5} \div \frac{1}{4} = \frac{8}{5}$ **or** $1\frac{3}{5}$

23) $1 \div \frac{4}{5} = \frac{5}{4}$ **or** $1\frac{1}{4}$

24) $\frac{1}{2} \div \frac{1}{4} = $ **2**

25) $\frac{3}{4} \div \frac{1}{2} = \frac{3}{2}$ **or** $1\frac{1}{2}$

26) $\frac{1}{5} \div \frac{2}{3} = \frac{3}{10}$

27) $\frac{3}{4} \div \frac{1}{4} = $ **3**

28) $\frac{1}{2} \div \frac{1}{2} = $ **1**

29) $\frac{1}{3} \div \frac{1}{3} = $ **1**

30) $\frac{2}{3} \div \frac{1}{3} = $ **2**

30/62

1) $5 \div \frac{13}{7} = \frac{35}{13}$ **or** $2\frac{9}{13}$

2) $3 \div \frac{19}{6} = \frac{18}{19}$

3) $\frac{15}{4} \div \frac{5}{3} = \frac{9}{4}$ **or** $2\frac{1}{4}$

4) $4 \div \frac{7}{2} = \frac{8}{7}$ **or** $1\frac{1}{7}$

5) $\frac{7}{2} \div \frac{5}{2} = \frac{7}{5}$ **or** $1\frac{2}{5}$

6) $4 \div \frac{25}{6} = \frac{24}{25}$

7) $\frac{8}{3} \div \frac{1}{4} = \frac{32}{3}$ **or** $10\frac{2}{3}$

8) $1 \div \frac{23}{8} = \frac{8}{23}$

9) $3 \div \frac{25}{7} = \frac{21}{25}$

10) $\frac{6}{5} \div \frac{9}{2} = \frac{4}{15}$

11) $\frac{1}{4} \div \frac{31}{7} = \frac{7}{124}$

12) $\frac{9}{2} \div \frac{13}{7} = \frac{63}{26}$ **or** $2\frac{11}{26}$

13) $\frac{9}{4} \div \frac{11}{2} = \frac{9}{22}$

14) $\frac{12}{5} \div 5 = \frac{12}{25}$

15) $\frac{2}{3} \div \frac{1}{2} = \frac{4}{3}$ **or** $1\frac{1}{3}$

31/62

16) $1 \div \frac{4}{3} = \frac{3}{4}$

17) $\frac{19}{4} \div \frac{17}{7} = \frac{133}{68}$ **or** $1\frac{65}{68}$

18) $\frac{7}{4} \div \frac{29}{7} = \frac{49}{116}$

19) $\frac{4}{5} \div \frac{25}{7} = \frac{28}{125}$

20) $2 \div \frac{1}{5} =$ **10**

21) $\frac{3}{2} \div \frac{16}{5} = \frac{15}{32}$

22) $\frac{8}{5} \div 5 = \frac{8}{25}$

23) $\frac{13}{5} \div 3 = \frac{13}{15}$

24) $1 \div \frac{5}{8} = \frac{8}{5}$ **or** $1\frac{3}{5}$

25) $\frac{17}{4} \div \frac{25}{8} = \frac{34}{25}$ **or** $1\frac{9}{25}$

26) $\frac{14}{5} \div \frac{2}{7} = \frac{49}{5}$ **or** $9\frac{4}{5}$

27) $\frac{7}{3} \div \frac{19}{4} = \frac{28}{57}$

28) $\frac{10}{3} \div \frac{1}{2} = \frac{20}{3}$ **or** $6\frac{2}{3}$

29) $\frac{1}{3} \div \frac{10}{7} = \frac{7}{30}$

30) $\frac{13}{5} \div \frac{29}{6} = \frac{78}{145}$

1) $\frac{10}{3} \div \frac{15}{7} = \frac{14}{9}$ **or** $1\frac{5}{9}$

2) $\frac{18}{5} \div \frac{1}{8} = \frac{144}{5}$ **or** $28\frac{4}{5}$

3) $\frac{9}{2} \div \frac{1}{2} =$ **9**

4) $\frac{9}{4} \div \frac{13}{5} = \frac{45}{52}$

5) $\frac{13}{4} \div \frac{17}{6} = \frac{39}{34}$ **or** $1\frac{5}{34}$

6) $4 \div \frac{15}{4} = \frac{16}{15}$ **or** $1\frac{1}{15}$

7) $\frac{7}{2} \div \frac{19}{7} = \frac{49}{38}$ **or** $1\frac{11}{38}$

8) $\frac{7}{3} \div 2 = \frac{7}{6}$ **or** $1\frac{1}{6}$

9) $3 \div \frac{18}{5} = \frac{5}{6}$

10) $\frac{5}{2} \div \frac{2}{7} = \frac{35}{4}$ **or** $8\frac{3}{4}$

11) $\frac{1}{3} \div \frac{7}{2} = \frac{2}{21}$

12) $2 \div \frac{10}{7} = \frac{7}{5}$ **or** $1\frac{2}{5}$

13) $\frac{1}{5} \div 2 = \frac{1}{10}$

14) $\frac{4}{3} \div \frac{17}{4} = \frac{16}{51}$

15) $\frac{7}{3} \div \frac{2}{5} = \frac{35}{6}$ **or** $5\frac{5}{6}$

32/62

16) $\frac{3}{2} \div 5 = \frac{3}{10}$

17) $\frac{21}{5} \div 3 = \frac{7}{5}$ **or** $1\frac{2}{5}$

18) $\frac{9}{2} \div \frac{21}{4} = \frac{6}{7}$

19) $\frac{1}{3} \div \frac{3}{4} = \frac{4}{9}$

20) $4 \div \frac{11}{3} = \frac{12}{11}$ **or** $1\frac{1}{11}$

21) $\frac{13}{4} \div \frac{13}{3} = \frac{3}{4}$

22) $\frac{8}{3} \div \frac{13}{4} = \frac{32}{39}$

23) $\frac{14}{3} \div \frac{9}{5} = \frac{70}{27}$ **or** $2\frac{16}{27}$

24) $3 \div \frac{5}{2} = \frac{6}{5}$ **or** $1\frac{1}{5}$

25) $\frac{17}{5} \div \frac{15}{8} = \frac{136}{75}$ **or** $1\frac{61}{75}$

26) $\frac{14}{5} \div \frac{6}{5} = \frac{7}{3}$ **or** $2\frac{1}{3}$

27) $\frac{8}{5} \div \frac{5}{2} = \frac{16}{25}$

28) $\frac{21}{4} \div \frac{25}{8} = \frac{42}{25}$ **or** $1\frac{17}{25}$

29) $\frac{3}{2} \div 1 = \frac{3}{2}$ **or** $1\frac{1}{2}$

30) $2 \div \frac{2}{5} =$ **5**

1) $\frac{5}{4} \div \frac{3}{2} = \frac{5}{6}$

2) $\frac{1}{2} \div \frac{13}{3} = \frac{3}{26}$

3) $5 \div \frac{17}{6} = \frac{30}{17}$ **or** $1\frac{13}{17}$

4) $\frac{3}{2} \div \frac{22}{7} = \frac{21}{44}$

5) $\frac{3}{2} \div \frac{24}{7} = \frac{7}{16}$

6) $2 \div \frac{17}{6} = \frac{12}{17}$

7) $\frac{2}{3} \div \frac{11}{3} = \frac{2}{11}$

8) $\frac{7}{2} \div \frac{13}{5} = \frac{35}{26}$ **or** $1\frac{9}{26}$

9) $\frac{5}{2} \div 2 = \frac{5}{4}$ **or** $1\frac{1}{4}$

10) $4 \div \frac{8}{3} = \frac{3}{2}$ **or** $1\frac{1}{2}$

11) $\frac{13}{4} \div \frac{29}{6} = \frac{39}{58}$

12) $\frac{1}{5} \div \frac{5}{8} = \frac{8}{25}$

13) $5 \div \frac{4}{5} = \frac{25}{4}$ **or** $6\frac{1}{4}$

14) $4 \div \frac{10}{7} = \frac{14}{5}$ **or** $2\frac{4}{5}$

15) $\frac{1}{2} \div \frac{17}{5} = \frac{5}{34}$

16) $\frac{17}{5} \div 1 = \frac{17}{5}$ **or** $3\frac{2}{5}$

17) $\frac{13}{4} \div \frac{9}{2} = \frac{13}{18}$

18) $\frac{13}{3} \div \frac{17}{7} = \frac{91}{51}$ **or** $1\frac{40}{51}$

19) $\frac{13}{4} \div \frac{5}{3} = \frac{39}{20}$ **or** $1\frac{19}{20}$

20) $\frac{2}{5} \div \frac{29}{7} = \frac{14}{145}$

21) $\frac{3}{2} \div \frac{35}{8} = \frac{12}{35}$

22) $1 \div \frac{25}{8} = \frac{8}{25}$

23) $2 \div \frac{11}{3} = \frac{6}{11}$

24) $5 \div \frac{4}{3} = \frac{15}{4}$ **or** $3\frac{3}{4}$

25) $\frac{1}{4} \div \frac{11}{5} = \frac{5}{44}$

26) $2 \div \frac{3}{5} = \frac{10}{3}$ **or** $3\frac{1}{3}$

27) $\frac{9}{2} \div 1 = \frac{9}{2}$ **or** $4\frac{1}{2}$

28) $5 \div \frac{16}{5} = \frac{25}{16}$ **or** $1\frac{9}{16}$

29) $\frac{5}{3} \div 5 = \frac{1}{3}$

30) $\frac{1}{3} \div \frac{3}{4} = \frac{4}{9}$

33/62

1) $\frac{16}{5} \div \frac{11}{3} = \frac{48}{55}$

2) $\frac{7}{3} \div \frac{19}{5} = \frac{35}{57}$

3) $\frac{1}{4} \div \frac{3}{2} = \frac{1}{6}$

4) $1 \div \frac{19}{4} = \frac{4}{19}$

5) $\frac{13}{4} \div \frac{17}{4} = \frac{13}{17}$

6) $\frac{10}{3} \div \frac{2}{3} = $ **5**

7) $\frac{11}{3} \div \frac{19}{4} = \frac{44}{57}$

8) $1 \div \frac{9}{5} = \frac{5}{9}$

9) $\frac{3}{5} \div \frac{1}{2} = \frac{6}{5}$ **or** $1\frac{1}{5}$

10) $\frac{3}{4} \div \frac{13}{3} = \frac{9}{52}$

11) $\frac{13}{5} \div \frac{16}{7} = \frac{91}{80}$ **or** $1\frac{11}{80}$

12) $\frac{24}{5} \div \frac{10}{3} = \frac{36}{25}$ **or** $1\frac{11}{25}$

13) $2 \div \frac{5}{3} = \frac{6}{5}$ **or** $1\frac{1}{5}$

14) $5 \div \frac{23}{8} = \frac{40}{23}$ **or** $1\frac{17}{23}$

15) $\frac{5}{2} \div 1 = \frac{5}{2}$ **or** $2\frac{1}{2}$

16) $\frac{17}{4} \div \frac{9}{4} = \frac{17}{9}$ **or** $1\frac{8}{9}$

17) $3 \div \frac{19}{6} = \frac{18}{19}$

18) $4 \div \frac{7}{5} = \frac{20}{7}$ **or** $2\frac{6}{7}$

19) $3 \div \frac{6}{7} = \frac{7}{2}$ **or** $3\frac{1}{2}$

20) $\frac{10}{3} \div \frac{9}{8} = \frac{80}{27}$ **or** $2\frac{26}{27}$

21) $\frac{4}{3} \div \frac{4}{7} = \frac{7}{3}$ **or** $2\frac{1}{3}$

22) $\frac{1}{3} \div \frac{1}{3} = $ **1**

23) $\frac{1}{2} \div 3 = \frac{1}{6}$

24) $\frac{2}{5} \div \frac{29}{6} = \frac{12}{145}$

25) $4 \div \frac{13}{4} = \frac{16}{13}$ **or** $1\frac{3}{13}$

26) $\frac{2}{3} \div 5 = \frac{2}{15}$

27) $\frac{19}{5} \div 4 = \frac{19}{20}$

28) $\frac{1}{2} \div 1 = \frac{1}{2}$

29) $\frac{1}{3} \div 4 = \frac{1}{12}$

30) $\frac{18}{5} \div \frac{32}{7} = \frac{63}{80}$

34/62

1) $\frac{7}{2} \div \frac{14}{3} = \frac{3}{4}$

2) $\frac{18}{5} \div 2 = \frac{9}{5}$ **or** $1\frac{4}{5}$

3) $\frac{22}{5} \div \frac{7}{2} = \frac{44}{35}$ **or** $1\frac{9}{35}$

4) $\frac{21}{5} \div \frac{5}{2} = \frac{42}{25}$ **or** $1\frac{17}{25}$

5) $\frac{1}{2} \div \frac{11}{5} = \frac{5}{22}$

6) $5 \div \frac{33}{8} = \frac{40}{33}$ **or** $1\frac{7}{33}$

7) $1 \div \frac{11}{5} = \frac{5}{11}$

8) $\frac{2}{3} \div \frac{7}{3} = \frac{2}{7}$

9) $\frac{7}{2} \div 2 = \frac{7}{4}$ **or** $1\frac{3}{4}$

10) $2 \div \frac{25}{6} = \frac{12}{25}$

11) $3 \div \frac{4}{3} = \frac{9}{4}$ **or** $2\frac{1}{4}$

12) $1 \div \frac{5}{4} = \frac{4}{5}$

13) $\frac{11}{5} \div 3 = \frac{11}{15}$

14) $\frac{1}{4} \div \frac{15}{4} = \frac{1}{15}$

15) $\frac{24}{5} \div \frac{16}{5} = \frac{3}{2}$ **or** $1\frac{1}{2}$

16) $\frac{10}{3} \div \frac{31}{8} = \frac{80}{93}$

17) $\frac{11}{2} \div \frac{7}{2} = \frac{11}{7}$ **or** $1\frac{4}{7}$

18) $\frac{1}{4} \div \frac{7}{3} = \frac{3}{28}$

19) $5 \div \frac{2}{7} = \frac{35}{2}$ **or** $17\frac{1}{2}$

20) $\frac{8}{3} \div \frac{5}{7} = \frac{56}{15}$ **or** $3\frac{11}{15}$

21) $\frac{9}{2} \div 2 = \frac{9}{4}$ **or** $2\frac{1}{4}$

22) $\frac{2}{3} \div \frac{12}{7} = \frac{7}{18}$

23) $4 \div \frac{1}{2} = \mathbf{8}$

24) $4 \div \frac{16}{7} = \frac{7}{4}$ **or** $1\frac{3}{4}$

25) $\frac{21}{5} \div \frac{27}{8} = \frac{56}{45}$ **or** $1\frac{11}{45}$

26) $\frac{5}{3} \div \frac{15}{4} = \frac{4}{9}$

27) $2 \div \frac{5}{2} = \frac{4}{5}$

28) $\frac{3}{4} \div 5 = \frac{3}{20}$

29) $\frac{7}{2} \div \frac{32}{7} = \frac{49}{64}$

30) $\frac{5}{2} \div \frac{3}{7} = \frac{35}{6}$ **or** $5\frac{5}{6}$

35/62

1) $\frac{2}{5} \div \frac{33}{7} = \frac{14}{165}$

2) $\frac{7}{3} \div \frac{7}{3} =$ **1**

3) $\frac{4}{5} \div 1 = \frac{4}{5}$

4) $2 \div \frac{1}{5} =$ **10**

5) $\frac{7}{4} \div 1 = \frac{7}{4}$ **or** $1\frac{3}{4}$

6) $\frac{5}{2} \div \frac{2}{3} = \frac{15}{4}$ **or** $3\frac{3}{4}$

7) $1 \div \frac{7}{6} = \frac{6}{7}$

8) $\frac{1}{3} \div \frac{18}{5} = \frac{5}{54}$

9) $1 \div \frac{17}{7} = \frac{7}{17}$

10) $\frac{6}{5} \div \frac{16}{5} = \frac{3}{8}$

11) $\frac{17}{5} \div \frac{13}{4} = \frac{68}{65}$ **or** $1\frac{3}{65}$

12) $\frac{14}{5} \div 4 = \frac{7}{10}$

13) $\frac{11}{2} \div \frac{17}{4} = \frac{22}{17}$ **or** $1\frac{5}{17}$

14) $\frac{8}{5} \div \frac{22}{5} = \frac{4}{11}$

15) $\frac{7}{2} \div \frac{7}{2} =$ **1**

16) $\frac{2}{3} \div 2 = \frac{1}{3}$

17) $5 \div \frac{13}{6} = \frac{30}{13}$ **or** $2\frac{4}{13}$

18) $\frac{15}{4} \div 2 = \frac{15}{8}$ **or** $1\frac{7}{8}$

19) $3 \div \frac{1}{5} =$ **15**

20) $4 \div \frac{24}{5} = \frac{5}{6}$

21) $\frac{8}{5} \div 2 = \frac{4}{5}$

22) $\frac{7}{2} \div \frac{7}{4} =$ **2**

23) $2 \div \frac{22}{7} = \frac{7}{11}$

24) $\frac{3}{5} \div \frac{3}{4} = \frac{4}{5}$

25) $\frac{2}{3} \div \frac{5}{4} = \frac{8}{15}$

26) $\frac{9}{2} \div \frac{3}{4} =$ **6**

27) $1 \div \frac{7}{2} = \frac{2}{7}$

28) $\frac{1}{2} \div 5 = \frac{1}{10}$

29) $\frac{10}{3} \div \frac{1}{8} = \frac{80}{3}$ **or** $26\frac{2}{3}$

30) $2 \div \frac{8}{3} = \frac{3}{4}$

36/62

1) $\frac{1}{3} \div 3 = \frac{1}{9}$

2) $\frac{15}{4} \div 2 = \frac{15}{8}$ **or** $1\frac{7}{8}$

3) $1 \div \frac{5}{3} = \frac{3}{5}$

4) $\frac{13}{3} \div \frac{7}{3} = \frac{13}{7}$ **or** $1\frac{6}{7}$

5) $\frac{4}{3} \div \frac{6}{5} = \frac{10}{9}$ **or** $1\frac{1}{9}$

6) $2 \div \frac{17}{7} = \frac{14}{17}$

7) $1 \div \frac{2}{5} = \frac{5}{2}$ **or** $2\frac{1}{2}$

8) $\frac{7}{3} \div 4 = \frac{7}{12}$

9) $\frac{7}{2} \div \frac{3}{2} = \frac{7}{3}$ **or** $2\frac{1}{3}$

10) $\frac{4}{3} \div \frac{4}{3} = $ **1**

11) $1 \div \frac{20}{7} = \frac{7}{20}$

12) $\frac{7}{3} \div \frac{11}{4} = \frac{28}{33}$

13) $\frac{3}{2} \div \frac{8}{7} = \frac{21}{16}$ **or** $1\frac{5}{16}$

14) $\frac{4}{5} \div \frac{3}{2} = \frac{8}{15}$

15) $4 \div \frac{3}{2} = \frac{8}{3}$ **or** $2\frac{2}{3}$

37/62

16) $\frac{23}{5} \div 1 = \frac{23}{5}$ **or** $4\frac{3}{5}$

17) $\frac{7}{3} \div \frac{4}{3} = \frac{7}{4}$ **or** $1\frac{3}{4}$

18) $4 \div \frac{1}{3} = $ **12**

19) $1 \div \frac{8}{5} = \frac{5}{8}$

20) $\frac{19}{4} \div 5 = \frac{19}{20}$

21) $\frac{23}{5} \div \frac{7}{2} = \frac{46}{35}$ **or** $1\frac{11}{35}$

22) $5 \div \frac{13}{3} = \frac{15}{13}$ **or** $1\frac{2}{13}$

23) $\frac{3}{2} \div \frac{8}{3} = \frac{9}{16}$

24) $\frac{10}{3} \div \frac{33}{7} = \frac{70}{99}$

25) $\frac{7}{3} \div \frac{9}{4} = \frac{28}{27}$ **or** $1\frac{1}{27}$

26) $2 \div \frac{12}{5} = \frac{5}{6}$

27) $2 \div \frac{22}{5} = \frac{5}{11}$

28) $3 \div \frac{7}{4} = \frac{12}{7}$ **or** $1\frac{5}{7}$

29) $\frac{1}{2} \div \frac{3}{2} = \frac{1}{3}$

30) $\frac{24}{5} \div \frac{19}{4} = \frac{96}{95}$ **or** $1\frac{1}{95}$

1) $\frac{1}{2} \div \frac{4}{7} = \frac{7}{8}$

2) $\frac{4}{5} \div \frac{1}{8} = \frac{32}{5}$ **or** $6\frac{2}{5}$

3) $\frac{1}{6} \div \frac{2}{3} = \frac{1}{4}$

4) $\frac{1}{5} \div \frac{6}{7} = \frac{7}{30}$

5) $\frac{3}{4} \div \frac{4}{5} = \frac{15}{16}$

6) $\frac{3}{5} \div \frac{3}{10} = $ **2**

7) $\frac{2}{5} \div \frac{5}{6} = \frac{12}{25}$

8) $\frac{2}{3} \div \frac{1}{2} = \frac{4}{3}$ **or** $1\frac{1}{3}$

9) $\frac{3}{7} \div \frac{1}{2} = \frac{6}{7}$

10) $\frac{3}{4} \div \frac{1}{2} = \frac{3}{2}$ **or** $1\frac{1}{2}$

11) $\frac{1}{5} \div \frac{1}{3} = \frac{3}{5}$

12) $\frac{1}{2} \div \frac{1}{2} = $ **1**

13) $\frac{1}{3} \div \frac{4}{5} = \frac{5}{12}$

14) $\frac{5}{6} \div \frac{2}{3} = \frac{5}{4}$ **or** $1\frac{1}{4}$

15) $\frac{1}{3} \div \frac{6}{7} = \frac{7}{18}$

16) $\frac{5}{6} \div \frac{1}{2} = \frac{5}{3}$ **or** $1\frac{2}{3}$

17) $\frac{1}{8} \div \frac{2}{3} = \frac{3}{16}$

18) $\frac{8}{9} \div \frac{8}{9} = $ **1**

19) $\frac{5}{6} \div \frac{1}{2} = \frac{5}{3}$ **or** $1\frac{2}{3}$

20) $\frac{4}{5} \div \frac{3}{4} = \frac{16}{15}$ **or** $1\frac{1}{15}$

21) $\frac{1}{2} \div \frac{1}{3} = \frac{3}{2}$ **or** $1\frac{1}{2}$

22) $\frac{1}{4} \div \frac{6}{7} = \frac{7}{24}$

23) $\frac{4}{5} \div \frac{1}{2} = \frac{8}{5}$ **or** $1\frac{3}{5}$

24) $\frac{2}{3} \div \frac{5}{7} = \frac{14}{15}$

25) $\frac{2}{3} \div \frac{2}{5} = \frac{5}{3}$ **or** $1\frac{2}{3}$

26) $\frac{4}{5} \div \frac{1}{4} = \frac{16}{5}$ **or** $3\frac{1}{5}$

27) $\frac{1}{5} \div \frac{5}{7} = \frac{7}{25}$

28) $\frac{3}{5} \div \frac{1}{3} = \frac{9}{5}$ **or** $1\frac{4}{5}$

29) $\frac{1}{2} \div \frac{1}{4} = $ **2**

30) $\frac{4}{5} \div \frac{3}{4} = \frac{16}{15}$ **or** $1\frac{1}{15}$

38/62

1) $\frac{7}{9} \div \frac{5}{7} = \frac{49}{45}$ **or** $1\frac{4}{45}$

2) $\frac{7}{10} \div \frac{1}{2} = \frac{7}{5}$ **or** $1\frac{2}{5}$

3) $\frac{1}{8} \div \frac{5}{6} = \frac{3}{20}$

4) $\frac{1}{3} \div \frac{3}{8} = \frac{8}{9}$

5) $\frac{1}{3} \div \frac{1}{2} = \frac{2}{3}$

6) $\frac{1}{6} \div \frac{1}{2} = \frac{1}{3}$

7) $\frac{7}{8} \div 1 = \frac{7}{8}$

8) $\frac{7}{8} \div \frac{2}{5} = \frac{35}{16}$ **or** $2\frac{3}{16}$

9) $\frac{1}{3} \div \frac{3}{5} = \frac{5}{9}$

10) $\frac{2}{9} \div \frac{1}{2} = \frac{4}{9}$

11) $\frac{1}{2} \div \frac{1}{5} = \frac{5}{2}$ **or** $2\frac{1}{2}$

12) $\frac{3}{10} \div \frac{5}{7} = \frac{21}{50}$

13) $\frac{2}{3} \div \frac{3}{4} = \frac{8}{9}$

14) $\frac{1}{2} \div \frac{1}{7} = \frac{7}{2}$ **or** $3\frac{1}{2}$

15) $\frac{1}{3} \div \frac{1}{7} = \frac{7}{3}$ **or** $2\frac{1}{3}$

39/62

16) $\frac{1}{2} \div \frac{1}{4} = $ **2**

17) $\frac{5}{6} \div \frac{7}{9} = \frac{15}{14}$ **or** $1\frac{1}{14}$

18) $\frac{1}{2} \div \frac{2}{3} = \frac{3}{4}$

19) $\frac{1}{2} \div \frac{3}{8} = \frac{4}{3}$ **or** $1\frac{1}{3}$

20) $\frac{2}{5} \div \frac{5}{6} = \frac{12}{25}$

21) $\frac{1}{4} \div \frac{4}{5} = \frac{5}{16}$

22) $\frac{1}{2} \div \frac{2}{3} = \frac{3}{4}$

23) $\frac{2}{5} \div \frac{1}{2} = \frac{4}{5}$

24) $\frac{1}{2} \div \frac{3}{5} = \frac{5}{6}$

25) $\frac{1}{5} \div \frac{1}{2} = \frac{2}{5}$

26) $\frac{3}{5} \div \frac{1}{2} = \frac{6}{5}$ **or** $1\frac{1}{5}$

27) $\frac{6}{7} \div \frac{2}{5} = \frac{15}{7}$ **or** $2\frac{1}{7}$

28) $\frac{3}{10} \div \frac{5}{9} = \frac{27}{50}$

29) $\frac{1}{2} \div \frac{3}{5} = \frac{5}{6}$

30) $\frac{6}{7} \div \frac{1}{3} = \frac{18}{7}$ **or** $2\frac{4}{7}$

1) $\frac{1}{2} \div \frac{2}{5} = \frac{5}{4}$ **or** $1\frac{1}{4}$

2) $\frac{1}{3} \div \frac{1}{3} = $ **1**

3) $\frac{9}{10} \div \frac{1}{3} = \frac{27}{10}$ **or** $2\frac{7}{10}$

4) $\frac{6}{7} \div \frac{5}{6} = \frac{36}{35}$ **or** $1\frac{1}{35}$

5) $\frac{1}{2} \div \frac{3}{10} = \frac{5}{3}$ **or** $1\frac{2}{3}$

6) $\frac{3}{4} \div \frac{1}{4} = $ **3**

7) $\frac{3}{8} \div \frac{5}{6} = \frac{9}{20}$

8) $\frac{4}{9} \div \frac{1}{5} = \frac{20}{9}$ **or** $2\frac{2}{9}$

9) $\frac{3}{10} \div \frac{2}{3} = \frac{9}{20}$

10) $\frac{1}{3} \div \frac{4}{5} = \frac{5}{12}$

11) $\frac{1}{10} \div \frac{1}{3} = \frac{3}{10}$

12) $\frac{5}{7} \div \frac{1}{2} = \frac{10}{7}$ **or** $1\frac{3}{7}$

13) $\frac{1}{2} \div \frac{1}{2} = $ **1**

14) $\frac{2}{7} \div \frac{6}{7} = \frac{1}{3}$

15) $\frac{1}{2} \div \frac{1}{3} = \frac{3}{2}$ **or** $1\frac{1}{2}$

40/62

16) $\frac{3}{5} \div \frac{1}{2} = \frac{6}{5}$ **or** $1\frac{1}{5}$

17) $\frac{1}{2} \div \frac{1}{3} = \frac{3}{2}$ **or** $1\frac{1}{2}$

18) $\frac{5}{8} \div \frac{1}{2} = \frac{5}{4}$ **or** $1\frac{1}{4}$

19) $\frac{2}{3} \div \frac{5}{6} = \frac{4}{5}$

20) $\frac{1}{4} \div \frac{3}{7} = \frac{7}{12}$

21) $\frac{4}{5} \div \frac{1}{9} = \frac{36}{5}$ **or** $7\frac{1}{5}$

22) $\frac{4}{7} \div \frac{4}{5} = \frac{5}{7}$

23) $\frac{2}{3} \div \frac{2}{5} = \frac{5}{3}$ **or** $1\frac{2}{3}$

24) $\frac{3}{7} \div \frac{5}{6} = \frac{18}{35}$

25) $\frac{4}{5} \div \frac{2}{3} = \frac{6}{5}$ **or** $1\frac{1}{5}$

26) $\frac{2}{3} \div \frac{1}{7} = \frac{14}{3}$ **or** $4\frac{2}{3}$

27) $\frac{1}{3} \div 1 = \frac{1}{3}$

28) $\frac{1}{2} \div \frac{2}{3} = \frac{3}{4}$

29) $\frac{4}{5} \div \frac{3}{4} = \frac{16}{15}$ **or** $1\frac{1}{15}$

30) $\frac{2}{5} \div \frac{4}{5} = \frac{1}{2}$

1) $\frac{6}{7} \div \frac{3}{8} = \frac{16}{7}$ **or** $2\frac{2}{7}$

2) $\frac{7}{8} \times \frac{1}{2} = \frac{7}{16}$

3) $\frac{2}{5} \div \frac{1}{6} = \frac{12}{5}$ **or** $2\frac{2}{5}$

4) $\frac{5}{6} \times \frac{1}{6} = \frac{5}{36}$

5) $\frac{3}{5} \times \frac{5}{6} = \frac{1}{2}$

6) $\frac{2}{5} \div \frac{1}{6} = \frac{12}{5}$ **or** $2\frac{2}{5}$

7) $\frac{3}{4} \div \frac{1}{4} = \mathbf{3}$

8) $\frac{1}{3} \times \frac{2}{5} = \frac{2}{15}$

9) $\frac{3}{5} \times \frac{4}{5} = \frac{12}{25}$

10) $\frac{5}{6} \div \frac{4}{5} = \frac{25}{24}$ **or** $1\frac{1}{24}$

11) $\frac{7}{9} \times \frac{2}{7} = \frac{2}{9}$

12) $\frac{1}{5} \div \frac{8}{9} = \frac{9}{40}$

13) $\frac{7}{8} \div \frac{2}{5} = \frac{35}{16}$ **or** $2\frac{3}{16}$

14) $\frac{5}{9} \div \frac{1}{3} = \frac{5}{3}$ **or** $1\frac{2}{3}$

41/62

15) $\frac{5}{6} \times \frac{1}{3} = \frac{5}{18}$

16) $\frac{2}{9} \times \frac{1}{3} = \frac{2}{27}$

17) $\frac{2}{3} \times \frac{2}{7} = \frac{4}{21}$

18) $\frac{2}{9} \times \frac{1}{2} = \frac{1}{9}$

19) $\frac{5}{9} \div \frac{3}{4} = \frac{20}{27}$

20) $\frac{1}{2} \div \frac{4}{5} = \frac{5}{8}$

21) $\frac{1}{2} \times \frac{1}{6} = \frac{1}{12}$

22) $\frac{3}{4} \div \frac{4}{7} = \frac{21}{16}$ **or** $1\frac{5}{16}$

23) $\frac{1}{8} \div \frac{1}{2} = \frac{1}{4}$

24) $\frac{2}{3} \times \frac{5}{8} = \frac{5}{12}$

25) $\frac{6}{7} \times \frac{7}{9} = \frac{2}{3}$

26) $\frac{7}{9} \times \frac{2}{7} = \frac{2}{9}$

27) $\frac{1}{4} \div \frac{1}{4} = \mathbf{1}$

28) $\frac{4}{7} \div \frac{1}{9} = \frac{36}{7}$ **or** $5\frac{1}{7}$

29) $\frac{1}{3} \times \frac{1}{5} = \frac{1}{15}$

30) $\frac{3}{4} \div \frac{8}{9} = \frac{27}{32}$

1) $\frac{2}{3}$ x $\frac{3}{8}$ = $\frac{1}{4}$

2) $\frac{7}{10}$ x $\frac{2}{3}$ = $\frac{7}{15}$

3) $\frac{3}{4}$ ÷ $\frac{1}{2}$ = $\frac{3}{2}$ **or** $1\frac{1}{2}$

4) $\frac{1}{3}$ ÷ $\frac{1}{3}$ = **1**

5) $\frac{1}{6}$ x $\frac{1}{2}$ = $\frac{1}{12}$

6) $\frac{3}{4}$ x $\frac{1}{2}$ = $\frac{3}{8}$

7) $\frac{1}{9}$ ÷ $\frac{2}{3}$ = $\frac{1}{6}$

8) $\frac{5}{7}$ ÷ $\frac{2}{3}$ = $\frac{15}{14}$ **or** $1\frac{1}{14}$

9) $\frac{8}{9}$ x $\frac{2}{3}$ = $\frac{16}{27}$

10) $\frac{8}{9}$ x $\frac{5}{7}$ = $\frac{40}{63}$

11) $\frac{3}{4}$ ÷ $\frac{1}{2}$ = $\frac{3}{2}$ **or** $1\frac{1}{2}$

12) $\frac{2}{3}$ ÷ $\frac{1}{5}$ = $\frac{10}{3}$ **or** $3\frac{1}{3}$

13) $\frac{1}{5}$ x $\frac{2}{3}$ = $\frac{2}{15}$

14) $\frac{1}{2}$ x $\frac{2}{3}$ = $\frac{1}{3}$

15) $\frac{4}{7}$ ÷ $\frac{8}{9}$ = $\frac{9}{14}$

16) $\frac{1}{4}$ ÷ $\frac{3}{4}$ = $\frac{1}{3}$

17) $\frac{1}{5}$ ÷ $\frac{1}{4}$ = $\frac{4}{5}$

18) $\frac{1}{7}$ x $\frac{2}{3}$ = $\frac{2}{21}$

19) 1 ÷ $\frac{1}{2}$ = **2**

20) $\frac{1}{6}$ x $\frac{4}{5}$ = $\frac{2}{15}$

21) $\frac{1}{7}$ ÷ $\frac{3}{8}$ = $\frac{8}{21}$

22) $\frac{3}{4}$ ÷ $\frac{2}{3}$ = $\frac{9}{8}$ **or** $1\frac{1}{8}$

23) $\frac{3}{4}$ x $\frac{9}{10}$ = $\frac{27}{40}$

24) $\frac{1}{9}$ x $\frac{1}{2}$ = $\frac{1}{18}$

25) $\frac{4}{5}$ ÷ $\frac{3}{5}$ = $\frac{4}{3}$ **or** $1\frac{1}{3}$

26) $\frac{2}{3}$ x $\frac{1}{2}$ = $\frac{1}{3}$

27) $\frac{7}{8}$ ÷ $\frac{1}{10}$ = $\frac{35}{4}$ **or** $8\frac{3}{4}$

28) $\frac{4}{7}$ x $\frac{1}{2}$ = $\frac{2}{7}$

29) $\frac{6}{7}$ x $\frac{2}{3}$ = $\frac{4}{7}$

30) $\frac{1}{8}$ x $\frac{5}{6}$ = $\frac{5}{48}$

42/62

1) $\frac{6}{7} \div \frac{1}{4} = \frac{24}{7}$ **or** $3\frac{3}{7}$

2) $\frac{1}{7} \times \frac{1}{2} = \frac{1}{14}$

3) $\frac{5}{7} \times \frac{1}{2} = \frac{5}{14}$

4) $\frac{1}{4} \div \frac{2}{3} = \frac{3}{8}$

5) $\frac{5}{6} \div \frac{7}{8} = \frac{20}{21}$

6) $\frac{2}{7} \times \frac{1}{3} = \frac{2}{21}$

7) $\frac{5}{7} \times \frac{2}{5} = \frac{2}{7}$

8) $\frac{7}{8} \div \frac{2}{5} = \frac{35}{16}$ **or** $2\frac{3}{16}$

9) $\frac{1}{2} \div \frac{2}{3} = \frac{3}{4}$

10) $\frac{3}{4} \times \frac{1}{2} = \frac{3}{8}$

11) $\frac{5}{6} \div \frac{1}{2} = \frac{5}{3}$ **or** $1\frac{2}{3}$

12) $\frac{1}{4} \times \frac{2}{3} = \frac{1}{6}$

13) $\frac{1}{2} \times \frac{7}{10} = \frac{7}{20}$

14) $\frac{2}{5} \div \frac{7}{10} = \frac{4}{7}$

15) $\frac{4}{9} \div \frac{3}{5} = \frac{20}{27}$

43/62

16) $\frac{6}{7} \times \frac{1}{2} = \frac{3}{7}$

17) $\frac{4}{5} \div \frac{4}{5} = $ **1**

18) $\frac{1}{2} \times \frac{1}{2} = \frac{1}{4}$

19) $\frac{1}{3} \div \frac{1}{3} = $ **1**

20) $\frac{4}{9} \times \frac{4}{5} = \frac{16}{45}$

21) $\frac{1}{6} \times \frac{3}{5} = \frac{1}{10}$

22) $\frac{3}{4} \times \frac{2}{3} = \frac{1}{2}$

23) $\frac{4}{9} \div \frac{1}{2} = \frac{8}{9}$

24) $\frac{1}{2} \div \frac{2}{5} = \frac{5}{4}$ **or** $1\frac{1}{4}$

25) $\frac{7}{9} \div \frac{1}{4} = \frac{28}{9}$ **or** $3\frac{1}{9}$

26) $\frac{3}{4} \times \frac{1}{2} = \frac{3}{8}$

27) $\frac{7}{10} \times \frac{1}{2} = \frac{7}{20}$

28) $\frac{1}{9} \div \frac{3}{7} = \frac{7}{27}$

29) $\frac{3}{4} \div \frac{1}{3} = \frac{9}{4}$ **or** $2\frac{1}{4}$

30) $\frac{7}{8} \times \frac{1}{4} = \frac{7}{32}$

1) $\frac{1}{4} \times \frac{4}{5} = \frac{1}{5}$

2) $\frac{1}{2} \div \frac{1}{2} =$ **1**

3) $\frac{1}{5} \div \frac{1}{2} = \frac{2}{5}$

4) $1 \times \frac{1}{3} = \frac{1}{3}$

5) $\frac{1}{2} \div \frac{1}{2} =$ **1**

6) $\frac{1}{3} \div \frac{1}{5} = \frac{5}{3}$ **or** $1\frac{2}{3}$

7) $\frac{2}{9} \times \frac{1}{4} = \frac{1}{18}$

8) $\frac{4}{7} \times \frac{3}{8} = \frac{3}{14}$

9) $\frac{3}{4} \times \frac{1}{2} = \frac{3}{8}$

10) $\frac{2}{7} \times \frac{5}{8} = \frac{5}{28}$

11) $\frac{2}{5} \div \frac{1}{3} = \frac{6}{5}$ **or** $1\frac{1}{5}$

12) $\frac{1}{2} \div \frac{5}{7} = \frac{7}{10}$

13) $\frac{1}{2} \div \frac{4}{5} = \frac{5}{8}$

14) $\frac{7}{10} \times \frac{7}{8} = \frac{49}{80}$

15) $\frac{1}{5} \times \frac{2}{3} = \frac{2}{15}$

16) $\frac{3}{4} \div \frac{1}{4} =$ **3**

17) $\frac{9}{10} \div \frac{1}{3} = \frac{27}{10}$ **or** $2\frac{7}{10}$

18) $\frac{7}{10} \div \frac{1}{2} = \frac{7}{5}$ **or** $1\frac{2}{5}$

19) $\frac{2}{3} \times \frac{1}{4} = \frac{1}{6}$

20) $\frac{2}{5} \times \frac{1}{2} = \frac{1}{5}$

21) $\frac{2}{3} \div \frac{2}{3} =$ **1**

22) $\frac{1}{2} \div \frac{1}{7} = \frac{7}{2}$ **or** $3\frac{1}{2}$

23) $\frac{2}{3} \times \frac{2}{3} = \frac{4}{9}$

24) $\frac{1}{2} \times \frac{3}{4} = \frac{3}{8}$

25) $\frac{1}{3} \times \frac{1}{3} = \frac{1}{9}$

26) $\frac{1}{5} \div \frac{4}{5} = \frac{1}{4}$

27) $\frac{7}{9} \div \frac{3}{5} = \frac{35}{27}$ **or** $1\frac{8}{27}$

28) $\frac{2}{3} \times \frac{1}{2} = \frac{1}{3}$

29) $\frac{3}{4} \div \frac{1}{6} = \frac{9}{2}$ **or** $4\frac{1}{2}$

30) $\frac{1}{2} \times \frac{4}{5} = \frac{2}{5}$

44/62

1) $\frac{1}{8} \div \frac{1}{2} = \frac{1}{4}$

2) $\frac{1}{2} \times \frac{1}{3} = \frac{1}{6}$

3) $\frac{1}{3} \times \frac{2}{7} = \frac{2}{21}$

4) $\frac{3}{10} \div \frac{2}{5} = \frac{3}{4}$

5) $\frac{4}{5} \times \frac{3}{4} = \frac{3}{5}$

6) $\frac{1}{2} \div \frac{1}{5} = \frac{5}{2}$ **or** $2\frac{1}{2}$

7) $\frac{1}{6} \div \frac{2}{5} = \frac{5}{12}$

8) $\frac{5}{6} \times \frac{1}{2} = \frac{5}{12}$

9) $\frac{5}{8} \div \frac{1}{2} = \frac{5}{4}$ **or** $1\frac{1}{4}$

10) $\frac{1}{2} \div \frac{3}{7} = \frac{7}{6}$ **or** $1\frac{1}{6}$

11) $\frac{3}{4} \times \frac{1}{5} = \frac{3}{20}$

12) $\frac{1}{2} \times \frac{1}{3} = \frac{1}{6}$

13) $\frac{2}{3} \div \frac{1}{4} = \frac{8}{3}$ **or** $2\frac{2}{3}$

14) $\frac{5}{6} \times \frac{1}{2} = \frac{5}{12}$

15) $\frac{1}{2} \times \frac{3}{5} = \frac{3}{10}$

16) $\frac{1}{2} \div \frac{1}{5} = \frac{5}{2}$ **or** $2\frac{1}{2}$

17) $\frac{1}{2} \times \frac{2}{5} = \frac{1}{5}$

18) $\frac{4}{7} \times 1 = \frac{4}{7}$

19) $\frac{3}{8} \div \frac{2}{5} = \frac{15}{16}$

20) $\frac{1}{3} \div \frac{4}{9} = \frac{3}{4}$

21) $\frac{1}{2} \div \frac{1}{6} =$ **3**

22) $\frac{1}{6} \times \frac{2}{3} = \frac{1}{9}$

23) $\frac{1}{2} \div \frac{3}{7} = \frac{7}{6}$ **or** $1\frac{1}{6}$

24) $\frac{1}{2} \times \frac{1}{3} = \frac{1}{6}$

25) $\frac{4}{5} \times \frac{1}{2} = \frac{2}{5}$

26) $\frac{1}{2} \div \frac{1}{2} =$ **1**

27) $\frac{4}{7} \div \frac{3}{4} = \frac{16}{21}$

28) $\frac{4}{7} \times \frac{1}{4} = \frac{1}{7}$

29) $\frac{3}{4} \times \frac{3}{5} = \frac{9}{20}$

30) $\frac{2}{5} \times \frac{1}{2} = \frac{1}{5}$

45/62

1) $\frac{1}{5}$ x $\frac{1}{2}$ = $\frac{1}{10}$

2) $\frac{1}{2}$ ÷ $\frac{1}{3}$ = $\frac{3}{2}$ **or** $1\frac{1}{2}$

3) $\frac{7}{8}$ ÷ $\frac{1}{2}$ = $\frac{7}{4}$ **or** $1\frac{3}{4}$

4) $\frac{3}{4}$ x $\frac{5}{8}$ = $\frac{15}{32}$

5) $\frac{3}{4}$ x 1 = $\frac{3}{4}$

6) $\frac{1}{4}$ x $\frac{2}{5}$ = $\frac{1}{10}$

7) $\frac{1}{2}$ ÷ $\frac{5}{7}$ = $\frac{7}{10}$

8) $\frac{8}{9}$ ÷ $\frac{3}{8}$ = $\frac{64}{27}$ **or** $2\frac{10}{27}$

9) $\frac{1}{2}$ x $\frac{3}{4}$ = $\frac{3}{8}$

10) $\frac{5}{9}$ x $\frac{2}{3}$ = $\frac{10}{27}$

11) $\frac{1}{2}$ ÷ $\frac{2}{5}$ = $\frac{5}{4}$ **or** $1\frac{1}{4}$

12) $\frac{3}{4}$ ÷ $\frac{1}{2}$ = $\frac{3}{2}$ **or** $1\frac{1}{2}$

13) $\frac{3}{5}$ ÷ $\frac{1}{2}$ = $\frac{6}{5}$ **or** $1\frac{1}{5}$

14) $\frac{7}{10}$ x $\frac{5}{8}$ = $\frac{7}{16}$

15) $\frac{1}{4}$ x $\frac{3}{5}$ = $\frac{3}{20}$

46/62

16) $\frac{1}{3}$ ÷ $\frac{1}{2}$ = $\frac{2}{3}$

17) $\frac{4}{7}$ ÷ $\frac{2}{5}$ = $\frac{10}{7}$ **or** $1\frac{3}{7}$

18) $\frac{1}{5}$ x $\frac{1}{3}$ = $\frac{1}{15}$

19) $\frac{4}{5}$ x $\frac{2}{5}$ = $\frac{8}{25}$

20) $\frac{4}{5}$ ÷ $\frac{3}{8}$ = $\frac{32}{15}$ **or** $2\frac{2}{15}$

21) $\frac{1}{4}$ ÷ $\frac{1}{3}$ = $\frac{3}{4}$

22) $\frac{4}{9}$ x $\frac{6}{7}$ = $\frac{8}{21}$

23) $\frac{1}{3}$ ÷ $\frac{5}{7}$ = $\frac{7}{15}$

24) $\frac{3}{5}$ x $\frac{1}{2}$ = $\frac{3}{10}$

25) $\frac{1}{5}$ ÷ $\frac{7}{9}$ = $\frac{9}{35}$

26) $\frac{2}{3}$ x $\frac{2}{3}$ = $\frac{4}{9}$

27) $\frac{1}{2}$ x $\frac{4}{9}$ = $\frac{2}{9}$

28) $\frac{1}{4}$ ÷ $\frac{1}{4}$ = **1**

29) $\frac{5}{8}$ ÷ $\frac{1}{2}$ = $\frac{5}{4}$ **or** $1\frac{1}{4}$

30) $\frac{1}{2}$ ÷ $\frac{1}{3}$ = $\frac{3}{2}$ **or** $1\frac{1}{2}$

1) $\frac{7}{9} \div \frac{2}{3} = \frac{7}{6}$ **or** $1\frac{1}{6}$

2) $\frac{2}{3} \times \frac{6}{7} = \frac{4}{7}$

3) $\frac{7}{8} \div \frac{4}{7} = \frac{49}{32}$ **or** $1\frac{17}{32}$

4) $\frac{1}{9} \times \frac{2}{3} = \frac{2}{27}$

5) $\frac{1}{2} \div \frac{5}{6} = \frac{3}{5}$

6) $\frac{1}{8} \times \frac{1}{2} = \frac{1}{16}$

7) $\frac{1}{2} \div \frac{1}{4} = \mathbf{2}$

8) $\frac{6}{7} \times \frac{2}{5} = \frac{12}{35}$

9) $\frac{1}{2} \div \frac{1}{9} = \frac{9}{2}$ **or** $4\frac{1}{2}$

10) $\frac{3}{4} \times \frac{4}{9} = \frac{1}{3}$

11) $\frac{1}{4} \times \frac{3}{5} = \frac{3}{20}$

12) $\frac{1}{2} \div \frac{1}{2} = \mathbf{1}$

13) $\frac{1}{2} \times \frac{2}{3} = \frac{1}{3}$

14) $\frac{1}{4} \div \frac{2}{3} = \frac{3}{8}$

15) $\frac{1}{5} \div \frac{1}{5} = \mathbf{1}$

47/62

16) $\frac{2}{3} \times \frac{1}{3} = \frac{2}{9}$

17) $\frac{4}{5} \times \frac{1}{3} = \frac{4}{15}$

18) $\frac{4}{5} \div \frac{5}{6} = \frac{24}{25}$

19) $\frac{4}{5} \div \frac{1}{2} = \frac{8}{5}$ **or** $1\frac{3}{5}$

20) $\frac{6}{7} \times \frac{1}{3} = \frac{2}{7}$

21) $1 \times \frac{7}{10} = \frac{7}{10}$

22) $\frac{2}{3} \times \frac{1}{3} = \frac{2}{9}$

23) $\frac{1}{9} \div \frac{2}{3} = \frac{1}{6}$

24) $\frac{1}{2} \div \frac{1}{2} = \mathbf{1}$

25) $\frac{9}{10} \times \frac{1}{2} = \frac{9}{20}$

26) $\frac{4}{5} \div \frac{1}{2} = \frac{8}{5}$ **or** $1\frac{3}{5}$

27) $\frac{2}{5} \div \frac{1}{5} = \mathbf{2}$

28) $\frac{1}{5} \times \frac{1}{2} = \frac{1}{10}$

29) $\frac{2}{3} \times \frac{1}{4} = \frac{1}{6}$

30) $\frac{4}{7} \div \frac{3}{7} = \frac{4}{3}$ **or** $1\frac{1}{3}$

1) $\frac{3}{5} \times \frac{1}{10} = \frac{3}{50}$

2) $\frac{2}{3} \times \frac{3}{10} = \frac{1}{5}$

3) $\frac{1}{5} \div \frac{1}{2} = \frac{2}{5}$

4) $\frac{1}{3} \div \frac{1}{2} = \frac{2}{3}$

5) $\frac{1}{4} \div \frac{5}{6} = \frac{3}{10}$

6) $\frac{3}{5} \div \frac{2}{5} = \frac{3}{2}$ **or**

7) $\frac{1}{2} \times \frac{2}{3} = \frac{1}{3}$

8) $\frac{1}{3} \times \frac{1}{6} = \frac{1}{18}$

9) $\frac{1}{6} \div \frac{3}{5} = \frac{5}{18}$

10) $\frac{1}{5} \div 1 = \frac{1}{5}$

11) $\frac{1}{2} \times \frac{2}{3} = \frac{1}{3}$

12) $\frac{4}{5} \times \frac{1}{3} = \frac{4}{15}$

13) $\frac{2}{3} \div \frac{1}{2} = \frac{4}{3}$ **or** $1\frac{1}{3}$

14) $\frac{2}{3} \times \frac{4}{5} = \frac{8}{15}$

15) $\frac{1}{2} \div \frac{1}{7} = \frac{7}{2}$ **or** $3\frac{1}{2}$

48/62

16) $\frac{2}{3} \times \frac{1}{2} = \frac{1}{3}$

17) $\frac{2}{3} \times \frac{3}{4} = \frac{1}{2}$

18) $\frac{1}{3} \div \frac{1}{2} = \frac{2}{3}$

19) $\frac{4}{9} \div \frac{5}{9} = \frac{4}{5}$

20) $\frac{1}{2} \times \frac{1}{5} = \frac{1}{10}$

21) $\frac{2}{3} \div \frac{1}{2} = \frac{4}{3}$ **or** $1\frac{1}{3}$

22) $\frac{4}{5} \times \frac{4}{9} = \frac{16}{45}$

23) $\frac{3}{4} \times \frac{1}{2} = \frac{3}{8}$

24) $\frac{1}{10} \div \frac{2}{5} = \frac{1}{4}$

25) $\frac{3}{8} \div \frac{1}{5} = \frac{15}{8}$ **or** $1\frac{7}{8}$

26) $\frac{1}{2} \times \frac{8}{9} = \frac{4}{9}$

27) $\frac{1}{3} \div \frac{5}{6} = \frac{2}{5}$

28) $\frac{3}{4} \times \frac{1}{4} = \frac{3}{16}$

29) $\frac{1}{4} \div \frac{1}{4} = \mathbf{1}$

30) $\frac{1}{2} \times \frac{3}{4} = \frac{3}{8}$

1) $\frac{3}{4}$ x $\frac{1}{2}$ = $\frac{3}{8}$

2) $\frac{2}{3}$ ÷ $\frac{1}{5}$ = $\frac{10}{3}$ **or** $3\frac{1}{3}$

3) $\frac{8}{9}$ x $\frac{1}{2}$ = $\frac{4}{9}$

4) $\frac{3}{5}$ ÷ $\frac{2}{3}$ = $\frac{9}{10}$

5) $\frac{4}{5}$ x $\frac{2}{5}$ = $\frac{8}{25}$

6) $\frac{7}{9}$ x $\frac{1}{7}$ = $\frac{1}{9}$

7) $\frac{1}{3}$ ÷ 1 = $\frac{1}{3}$

8) $\frac{2}{3}$ ÷ $\frac{3}{5}$ = $\frac{10}{9}$ **or** $1\frac{1}{9}$

9) $\frac{1}{7}$ ÷ $\frac{5}{8}$ = $\frac{8}{35}$

10) $\frac{2}{7}$ ÷ $\frac{5}{7}$ = $\frac{2}{5}$

11) $\frac{3}{5}$ x $\frac{1}{7}$ = $\frac{3}{35}$

12) $\frac{1}{2}$ x $\frac{3}{5}$ = $\frac{3}{10}$

13) $\frac{1}{6}$ x $\frac{1}{3}$ = $\frac{1}{18}$

14) $\frac{4}{9}$ x $\frac{1}{7}$ = $\frac{4}{63}$

15) $\frac{2}{3}$ ÷ $\frac{1}{2}$ = $\frac{4}{3}$ **or** $1\frac{1}{3}$

49/62

16) $\frac{3}{4}$ ÷ $\frac{1}{3}$ = $\frac{9}{4}$ **or** $2\frac{1}{4}$

17) $\frac{7}{8}$ x $\frac{2}{5}$ = $\frac{7}{20}$

18) $\frac{6}{7}$ ÷ $\frac{1}{2}$ = $\frac{12}{7}$ **or** $1\frac{5}{7}$

19) $\frac{7}{8}$ ÷ $\frac{2}{5}$ = $\frac{35}{16}$ **or** $2\frac{3}{16}$

20) $\frac{3}{5}$ x $\frac{1}{4}$ = $\frac{3}{20}$

21) $\frac{9}{10}$ x $\frac{2}{3}$ = $\frac{3}{5}$

22) $\frac{1}{6}$ x $\frac{1}{2}$ = $\frac{1}{12}$

23) $\frac{3}{4}$ ÷ $\frac{2}{3}$ = $\frac{9}{8}$ **or** $1\frac{1}{8}$

24) $\frac{9}{10}$ ÷ $\frac{3}{5}$ = $\frac{3}{2}$ **or** $1\frac{1}{2}$

25) $\frac{2}{3}$ ÷ $\frac{1}{9}$ = **6**

26) $\frac{1}{2}$ x $\frac{4}{5}$ = $\frac{2}{5}$

27) $\frac{4}{5}$ ÷ $\frac{1}{5}$ = **4**

28) $\frac{1}{2}$ x $\frac{1}{10}$ = $\frac{1}{20}$

29) $\frac{4}{5}$ ÷ $\frac{1}{2}$ = $\frac{8}{5}$ **or** $1\frac{3}{5}$

30) $\frac{2}{5}$ x $\frac{3}{5}$ = $\frac{6}{25}$

1) $\frac{5}{7} \div \frac{1}{4} = \frac{20}{7}$ **or** $2\frac{6}{7}$

2) $\frac{2}{3} \times \frac{7}{10} = \frac{7}{15}$

3) $\frac{3}{4} \div \frac{1}{7} = \frac{21}{4}$ **or** $5\frac{1}{4}$

4) $\frac{3}{4} \times \frac{2}{5} = \frac{3}{10}$

5) $1 \div \frac{8}{9} = \frac{9}{8}$ **or** $1\frac{1}{8}$

6) $\frac{1}{2} \times \frac{3}{4} = \frac{3}{8}$

7) $\frac{5}{7} \div \frac{2}{3} = \frac{15}{14}$ **or** $1\frac{1}{14}$

8) $\frac{2}{5} \times \frac{2}{3} = \frac{4}{15}$

9) $\frac{3}{4} \times \frac{3}{5} = \frac{9}{20}$

10) $\frac{5}{7} \div \frac{2}{7} = \frac{5}{2}$ **or** $2\frac{1}{2}$

11) $\frac{7}{10} \times \frac{2}{9} = \frac{7}{45}$

12) $\frac{1}{9} \div \frac{2}{3} = \frac{1}{6}$

13) $\frac{2}{5} \times \frac{1}{2} = \frac{1}{5}$

14) $1 \div \frac{1}{2} = $ **2**

15) $\frac{1}{2} \div \frac{2}{5} = \frac{5}{4}$ **or** $1\frac{1}{4}$

50/62

16) $\frac{8}{9} \times \frac{4}{5} = \frac{32}{45}$

17) $\frac{2}{7} \times \frac{1}{8} = \frac{1}{28}$

18) $\frac{2}{5} \div \frac{4}{7} = \frac{7}{10}$

19) $\frac{1}{2} \div \frac{1}{3} = \frac{3}{2}$ **or** $1\frac{1}{2}$

20) $\frac{4}{5} \times \frac{1}{2} = \frac{2}{5}$

21) $\frac{2}{3} \times \frac{1}{2} = \frac{1}{3}$

22) $\frac{2}{7} \times \frac{1}{4} = \frac{1}{14}$

23) $\frac{1}{2} \div \frac{3}{5} = \frac{5}{6}$

24) $\frac{1}{8} \div \frac{1}{2} = \frac{1}{4}$

25) $\frac{1}{2} \div \frac{1}{4} = $ **2**

26) $\frac{9}{10} \times \frac{1}{4} = \frac{9}{40}$

27) $\frac{7}{8} \times \frac{1}{5} = \frac{7}{40}$

28) $\frac{2}{3} \div \frac{3}{10} = \frac{20}{9}$ **or** $2\frac{2}{9}$

29) $\frac{1}{6} \times \frac{5}{7} = \frac{5}{42}$

30) $\frac{1}{4} \div \frac{1}{2} = \frac{1}{2}$

1) $\frac{5}{9} \times \frac{3}{5} = \frac{1}{3}$

2) $\frac{2}{3} \times \frac{8}{9} = \frac{16}{27}$

3) $\frac{1}{3} \div \frac{9}{10} = \frac{10}{27}$

4) $\frac{1}{9} \div \frac{2}{7} = \frac{7}{18}$

5) $\frac{3}{8} \div \frac{5}{7} = \frac{21}{40}$

6) $\frac{1}{10} \times \frac{2}{3} = \frac{1}{15}$

7) $\frac{4}{5} \times \frac{1}{2} = \frac{2}{5}$

8) $\frac{1}{2} \div \frac{1}{2} =$ **1**

9) $\frac{2}{3} \times \frac{4}{7} = \frac{8}{21}$

10) $\frac{1}{2} \div \frac{4}{9} = \frac{9}{8}$ **or** $1\frac{1}{8}$

11) $\frac{2}{3} \div \frac{1}{2} = \frac{4}{3}$ **or** $1\frac{1}{3}$

12) $\frac{1}{10} \times \frac{1}{5} = \frac{1}{50}$

13) $\frac{4}{7} \times \frac{1}{3} = \frac{4}{21}$

14) $\frac{3}{7} \div \frac{3}{10} = \frac{10}{7}$ **or** $1\frac{3}{7}$

15) $\frac{7}{8} \div \frac{1}{2} = \frac{7}{4}$ **or** $1\frac{3}{4}$

16) $\frac{3}{4} \times \frac{1}{2} = \frac{3}{8}$

17) $\frac{5}{7} \div \frac{1}{5} = \frac{25}{7}$ **or** $3\frac{4}{7}$

18) $\frac{3}{8} \times \frac{1}{3} = \frac{1}{8}$

19) $\frac{1}{5} \div \frac{7}{8} = \frac{8}{35}$

20) $\frac{1}{2} \times \frac{1}{2} = \frac{1}{4}$

21) $\frac{1}{8} \div \frac{1}{9} = \frac{9}{8}$ **or** $1\frac{1}{8}$

22) $\frac{1}{4} \times \frac{4}{5} = \frac{1}{5}$

23) $\frac{1}{3} \times \frac{4}{5} = \frac{4}{15}$

24) $\frac{3}{4} \div \frac{1}{2} = \frac{3}{2}$ **or** $1\frac{1}{2}$

25) $\frac{2}{3} \times \frac{1}{2} = \frac{1}{3}$

26) $\frac{1}{5} \times \frac{2}{3} = \frac{2}{15}$

27) $\frac{1}{9} \div \frac{1}{2} = \frac{2}{9}$

28) $\frac{1}{7} \div \frac{2}{5} = \frac{5}{14}$

29) $\frac{2}{3} \div \frac{1}{2} = \frac{4}{3}$ **or** $1\frac{1}{3}$

30) $\frac{1}{3} \times \frac{1}{3} = \frac{1}{9}$

51/62

1) $\frac{2}{3} \times \frac{4}{5} = \frac{8}{15}$

2) $\frac{1}{2} \times \frac{1}{2} = \frac{1}{4}$

3) $\frac{9}{10} \div \frac{4}{5} = \frac{9}{8}$ **or** $1\frac{1}{8}$

4) $\frac{4}{5} \div \frac{1}{4} = \frac{16}{5}$ **or** $3\frac{1}{5}$

5) $\frac{1}{2} \div \frac{1}{2} = $ **1**

6) $\frac{4}{5} \times \frac{7}{9} = \frac{28}{45}$

7) $\frac{1}{2} \times \frac{2}{5} = \frac{1}{5}$

8) $\frac{3}{5} \div \frac{1}{5} = $ **3**

9) $\frac{2}{5} \times \frac{8}{9} = \frac{16}{45}$

10) $\frac{8}{9} \div \frac{1}{2} = \frac{16}{9}$ **or** $1\frac{7}{9}$

11) $\frac{1}{4} \times 1 = \frac{1}{4}$

12) $1 \div \frac{4}{7} = \frac{7}{4}$ **or** $1\frac{3}{4}$

13) $\frac{1}{4} \div \frac{1}{2} = \frac{1}{2}$

14) $\frac{1}{3} \div \frac{1}{2} = \frac{2}{3}$

15) $\frac{1}{6} \times \frac{3}{4} = \frac{1}{8}$

52/62

16) $\frac{1}{2} \times \frac{7}{9} = \frac{7}{18}$

17) $\frac{2}{3} \div \frac{5}{9} = \frac{6}{5}$ **or** $1\frac{1}{5}$

18) $\frac{2}{5} \times \frac{1}{2} = \frac{1}{5}$

19) $\frac{1}{3} \times \frac{1}{4} = \frac{1}{12}$

20) $\frac{6}{7} \div \frac{1}{5} = \frac{30}{7}$ **or** $4\frac{2}{7}$

21) $\frac{1}{4} \times \frac{5}{7} = \frac{5}{28}$

22) $\frac{3}{4} \times \frac{1}{7} = \frac{3}{28}$

23) $\frac{1}{2} \div \frac{4}{9} = \frac{9}{8}$ **or** $1\frac{1}{8}$

24) $\frac{1}{4} \div \frac{3}{8} = \frac{2}{3}$

25) $\frac{2}{5} \times \frac{1}{2} = \frac{1}{5}$

26) $\frac{1}{3} \times \frac{1}{2} = \frac{1}{6}$

27) $\frac{1}{4} \div \frac{7}{9} = \frac{9}{28}$

28) $\frac{1}{2} \div \frac{1}{6} = $ **3**

29) $\frac{4}{5} \times \frac{2}{3} = \frac{8}{15}$

30) $\frac{3}{7} \div \frac{2}{3} = \frac{9}{14}$

1) $\frac{1}{2}$ x $\frac{1}{8}$ = $\frac{1}{16}$

2) $\frac{3}{8}$ ÷ $\frac{7}{9}$ = $\frac{27}{56}$

3) $\frac{1}{10}$ ÷ $\frac{1}{7}$ = $\frac{7}{10}$

4) $\frac{4}{7}$ x $\frac{5}{8}$ = $\frac{5}{14}$

5) $\frac{3}{4}$ ÷ $\frac{1}{2}$ = $\frac{3}{2}$ **or** $1\frac{1}{2}$

6) $\frac{2}{5}$ x $\frac{7}{8}$ = $\frac{7}{20}$

7) $\frac{1}{4}$ ÷ $\frac{1}{7}$ = $\frac{7}{4}$ **or** $1\frac{3}{4}$

8) $\frac{2}{7}$ x $\frac{2}{3}$ = $\frac{4}{21}$

9) $\frac{1}{2}$ x $\frac{3}{10}$ = $\frac{3}{20}$

10) $\frac{2}{3}$ ÷ $\frac{3}{10}$ = $\frac{20}{9}$ **or** $2\frac{2}{9}$

11) $\frac{1}{2}$ x $\frac{7}{8}$ = $\frac{7}{16}$

12) $\frac{1}{2}$ ÷ $\frac{4}{9}$ = $\frac{9}{8}$ **or** $1\frac{1}{8}$

13) $\frac{1}{8}$ x $\frac{1}{2}$ = $\frac{1}{16}$

14) $\frac{1}{3}$ ÷ $\frac{1}{2}$ = $\frac{2}{3}$

15) $\frac{6}{7}$ ÷ $\frac{1}{2}$ = $\frac{12}{7}$ **or** $1\frac{5}{7}$

53/62

16) $\frac{4}{5}$ x $\frac{4}{9}$ = $\frac{16}{45}$

17) $\frac{2}{5}$ x $\frac{1}{3}$ = $\frac{2}{15}$

18) $\frac{1}{5}$ x $\frac{2}{7}$ = $\frac{2}{35}$

19) $\frac{2}{3}$ ÷ $\frac{1}{3}$ = **2**

20) $\frac{8}{9}$ ÷ $\frac{2}{3}$ = $\frac{4}{3}$ **or** $1\frac{1}{3}$

21) $\frac{1}{9}$ ÷ $\frac{2}{9}$ = $\frac{1}{2}$

22) $\frac{1}{3}$ x $\frac{1}{2}$ = $\frac{1}{6}$

23) $\frac{1}{2}$ x $\frac{3}{5}$ = $\frac{3}{10}$

24) $\frac{1}{5}$ ÷ $\frac{2}{5}$ = $\frac{1}{2}$

25) $\frac{8}{9}$ ÷ $\frac{1}{2}$ = $\frac{16}{9}$ **or** $1\frac{7}{9}$

26) $\frac{1}{2}$ x $\frac{1}{2}$ = $\frac{1}{4}$

27) $\frac{1}{2}$ ÷ $\frac{3}{4}$ = $\frac{2}{3}$

28) 1 x $\frac{5}{9}$ = $\frac{5}{9}$

29) $\frac{4}{7}$ x $\frac{1}{3}$ = $\frac{4}{21}$

30) $\frac{2}{5}$ ÷ $\frac{2}{7}$ = $\frac{7}{5}$ **or** $1\frac{2}{5}$

1) $\frac{4}{7} \div \frac{1}{2} = \frac{8}{7}$ **or** $1\frac{1}{7}$

2) $\frac{1}{2} \times \frac{3}{5} = \frac{3}{10}$

3) $\frac{2}{5} \div \frac{2}{7} = \frac{7}{5}$ **or** $1\frac{2}{5}$

4) $\frac{2}{5} \times \frac{1}{8} = \frac{1}{20}$

5) $\frac{1}{4} \times \frac{3}{10} = \frac{3}{40}$

6) $\frac{5}{6} \div \frac{1}{2} = \frac{5}{3}$ **or** $1\frac{2}{3}$

7) $\frac{6}{7} \times \frac{1}{7} = \frac{6}{49}$

8) $\frac{3}{4} \div \frac{1}{8} = \mathbf{6}$

9) $\frac{1}{10} \div \frac{2}{3} = \frac{3}{20}$

10) $\frac{3}{5} \times \frac{1}{5} = \frac{3}{25}$

11) $\frac{1}{6} \times \frac{1}{6} = \frac{1}{36}$

12) $\frac{5}{7} \div \frac{1}{2} = \frac{10}{7}$ **or** $1\frac{3}{7}$

13) $\frac{1}{5} \times \frac{5}{8} = \frac{1}{8}$

14) $\frac{1}{2} \div \frac{5}{8} = \frac{4}{5}$

15) $\frac{3}{7} \times \frac{1}{6} = \frac{1}{14}$

16) $\frac{1}{2} \div \frac{1}{2} = \mathbf{1}$

17) $\frac{1}{2} \times \frac{2}{3} = \frac{1}{3}$

18) $\frac{2}{7} \div \frac{4}{7} = \frac{1}{2}$

54/62

19) $\frac{1}{2} \div \frac{1}{3} = \frac{3}{2}$ **or** $1\frac{1}{2}$

20) $\frac{4}{9} \times \frac{3}{4} = \frac{1}{3}$

21) $\frac{1}{4} \times \frac{5}{9} = \frac{5}{36}$

22) $\frac{1}{2} \div \frac{3}{4} = \frac{2}{3}$

23) $\frac{7}{10} \div \frac{3}{4} = \frac{14}{15}$

24) $\frac{2}{3} \times \frac{1}{3} = \frac{2}{9}$

25) $\frac{4}{5} \div \frac{2}{3} = \frac{6}{5}$ **or** $1\frac{1}{5}$

26) $\frac{1}{4} \div \frac{3}{5} = \frac{5}{12}$

27) $\frac{3}{4} \times \frac{1}{3} = \frac{1}{4}$

28) $\frac{2}{5} \times \frac{3}{4} = \frac{3}{10}$

29) $\frac{1}{9} \div \frac{1}{5} = \frac{5}{9}$

30) $\frac{2}{3} \div \frac{1}{7} = \frac{14}{3}$ **or** $4\frac{2}{3}$

1) $\frac{5}{8} \times \frac{3}{10} = \frac{3}{16}$

2) $\frac{2}{3} \times \frac{1}{7} = \frac{2}{21}$

3) $\frac{1}{5} \div \frac{3}{5} = \frac{1}{3}$

4) $\frac{1}{3} \div \frac{1}{3} = \mathbf{1}$

5) $\frac{1}{8} \div \frac{2}{7} = \frac{7}{16}$

6) $\frac{1}{2} \times \frac{3}{8} = \frac{3}{16}$

7) $\frac{1}{2} \div \frac{5}{8} = \frac{4}{5}$

8) $\frac{3}{4} \times \frac{2}{7} = \frac{3}{14}$

9) $\frac{1}{3} \div \frac{3}{5} = \frac{5}{9}$

10) $\frac{1}{2} \times \frac{1}{2} = \frac{1}{4}$

11) $\frac{1}{5} \times \frac{4}{9} = \frac{4}{45}$

12) $\frac{2}{3} \div \frac{2}{5} = \frac{5}{3}$ **or** $1\frac{2}{3}$

13) $\frac{1}{2} \times \frac{1}{3} = \frac{1}{6}$

14) $\frac{2}{3} \div \frac{7}{8} = \frac{16}{21}$

15) $\frac{2}{3} \times \frac{1}{2} = \frac{1}{3}$

55/62

16) $\frac{1}{8} \div \frac{1}{2} = \frac{1}{4}$

17) $\frac{1}{4} \div \frac{3}{4} = \frac{1}{3}$

18) $\frac{1}{2} \times \frac{1}{2} = \frac{1}{4}$

19) $\frac{3}{5} \div \frac{1}{6} = \frac{18}{5}$ **or** $3\frac{3}{5}$

20) $\frac{5}{8} \times \frac{1}{2} = \frac{5}{16}$

21) $\frac{1}{2} \times \frac{1}{4} = \frac{1}{8}$

22) $\frac{8}{9} \div \frac{1}{7} = \frac{56}{9}$ **or** $6\frac{2}{9}$

23) $\frac{1}{9} \times \frac{1}{6} = \frac{1}{54}$

24) $\frac{1}{6} \div \frac{5}{8} = \frac{4}{15}$

25) $\frac{1}{2} \div \frac{1}{2} = \mathbf{1}$

26) $\frac{3}{5} \times \frac{1}{2} = \frac{3}{10}$

27) $\frac{1}{3} \times \frac{1}{2} = \frac{1}{6}$

28) $\frac{1}{2} \div \frac{1}{5} = \frac{5}{2}$ **or** $2\frac{1}{2}$

29) $\frac{2}{5} \div \frac{3}{4} = \frac{8}{15}$

30) $\frac{1}{4} \times \frac{3}{4} = \frac{3}{16}$

1) $\frac{4}{2}$ x $\frac{1}{2}$ = **1**

2) $\frac{5}{2}$ ÷ $\frac{9}{2}$ = $\frac{5}{9}$

3) $\frac{4}{7}$ ÷ $\frac{14}{7}$ = $\frac{2}{7}$

4) $\frac{12}{5}$ x $\frac{13}{5}$ = $\frac{156}{25}$ **or** $6\frac{6}{25}$

5) $\frac{19}{4}$ x $\frac{7}{4}$ = $\frac{133}{16}$ **or** $8\frac{5}{16}$

6) $\frac{16}{4}$ ÷ $\frac{11}{4}$ = $\frac{16}{11}$ **or** $1\frac{5}{11}$

7) $\frac{26}{8}$ ÷ $\frac{30}{8}$ = $\frac{13}{15}$

8) $\frac{5}{2}$ x $\frac{9}{2}$ = $\frac{45}{4}$ **or** $11\frac{1}{4}$

9) $\frac{4}{5}$ ÷ $\frac{2}{5}$ = **2**

10) $\frac{3}{2}$ x $\frac{3}{2}$ = $\frac{9}{4}$ **or** $2\frac{1}{4}$

11) $\frac{13}{5}$ ÷ $\frac{21}{5}$ = $\frac{13}{21}$

12) $\frac{19}{9}$ x $\frac{1}{9}$ = $\frac{19}{81}$

13) $\frac{9}{6}$ ÷ $\frac{8}{6}$ = $\frac{9}{8}$ **or** $1\frac{1}{8}$

14) $\frac{32}{7}$ x $\frac{12}{7}$ = $\frac{384}{49}$ **or** $7\frac{41}{49}$

15) $\frac{8}{7}$ x $\frac{12}{7}$ = $\frac{96}{49}$ **or** $1\frac{47}{49}$

56/62

16) $\frac{17}{7}$ ÷ $\frac{9}{7}$ = $\frac{17}{9}$ **or** $1\frac{8}{9}$

17) $\frac{15}{3}$ ÷ $\frac{8}{3}$ = $\frac{15}{8}$ **or** $1\frac{7}{8}$

18) $\frac{43}{9}$ x $\frac{28}{9}$ = $\frac{1204}{81}$ **or** $14\frac{70}{81}$

19) $\frac{16}{7}$ x $\frac{26}{7}$ = $\frac{416}{49}$ **or** $8\frac{24}{49}$

20) $\frac{8}{9}$ ÷ $\frac{1}{9}$ = **8**

21) $\frac{11}{6}$ x $\frac{11}{6}$ = $\frac{121}{36}$ **or** $3\frac{13}{36}$

22) $\frac{22}{5}$ ÷ $\frac{9}{5}$ = $\frac{22}{9}$ **or** $2\frac{4}{9}$

23) $\frac{13}{3}$ x $\frac{10}{3}$ = $\frac{130}{9}$ **or** $14\frac{4}{9}$

24) $\frac{6}{7}$ ÷ $\frac{29}{7}$ = $\frac{6}{29}$

25) $\frac{27}{8}$ ÷ $\frac{16}{8}$ = $\frac{27}{16}$ **or** $1\frac{11}{16}$

26) $\frac{32}{7}$ ÷ $\frac{4}{7}$ = **8**

27) $\frac{19}{10}$ x $\frac{9}{10}$ = $\frac{171}{100}$ **or** $1\frac{71}{100}$

28) $\frac{6}{5}$ x $\frac{3}{5}$ = $\frac{18}{25}$

29) $\frac{8}{9}$ ÷ $\frac{37}{9}$ = $\frac{8}{37}$

30) $\frac{7}{7}$ x $\frac{23}{7}$ = $\frac{23}{7}$ **or** $3\frac{2}{7}$

1) $\frac{13}{6}$ x $\frac{13}{6}$ = $\frac{169}{36}$ **or** $4\frac{25}{36}$

2) $\frac{18}{7}$ ÷ $\frac{24}{7}$ = $\frac{3}{4}$

3) $\frac{3}{4}$ x $\frac{7}{4}$ = $\frac{21}{16}$ **or** $1\frac{5}{16}$

4) $\frac{4}{3}$ ÷ $\frac{7}{3}$ = $\frac{4}{7}$

5) $\frac{4}{2}$ x $\frac{1}{2}$ = **1**

6) $\frac{30}{8}$ ÷ $\frac{26}{8}$ = $\frac{15}{13}$ **or** $1\frac{2}{13}$

7) $\frac{7}{4}$ x $\frac{13}{4}$ = $\frac{91}{16}$ **or** $5\frac{11}{16}$

8) $\frac{1}{10}$ ÷ $\frac{2}{10}$ = $\frac{1}{2}$

9) $\frac{3}{3}$ x $\frac{1}{3}$ = $\frac{1}{3}$

10) $\frac{3}{8}$ x $\frac{18}{8}$ = $\frac{27}{32}$

11) $\frac{3}{3}$ ÷ $\frac{2}{3}$ = $\frac{3}{2}$ **or** $1\frac{1}{2}$

12) $\frac{18}{10}$ ÷ $\frac{39}{10}$ = $\frac{6}{13}$

13) $\frac{7}{3}$ ÷ $\frac{13}{3}$ = $\frac{7}{13}$

14) $\frac{20}{7}$ ÷ $\frac{28}{7}$ = $\frac{5}{7}$

15) $\frac{35}{9}$ x $\frac{10}{9}$ = $\frac{350}{81}$ **or** $4\frac{26}{81}$

57/62

16) $\frac{2}{3}$ x $\frac{9}{3}$ = **2**

17) $\frac{3}{2}$ x $\frac{11}{2}$ = $\frac{33}{4}$ **or** $8\frac{1}{4}$

18) $\frac{7}{3}$ ÷ $\frac{13}{3}$ = $\frac{7}{13}$

19) $\frac{4}{9}$ ÷ $\frac{19}{9}$ = $\frac{4}{19}$

20) $\frac{4}{2}$ x $\frac{9}{2}$ = **9**

21) $\frac{7}{9}$ x $\frac{7}{9}$ = $\frac{49}{81}$

22) $\frac{15}{6}$ ÷ $\frac{2}{6}$ = $\frac{15}{2}$ **or** $7\frac{1}{2}$

23) $\frac{7}{2}$ x $\frac{6}{2}$ = $\frac{21}{2}$ **or** $10\frac{1}{2}$

24) $\frac{7}{6}$ ÷ $\frac{16}{6}$ = $\frac{7}{16}$

25) $\frac{3}{9}$ ÷ $\frac{36}{9}$ = $\frac{1}{12}$

26) $\frac{23}{5}$ x $\frac{18}{5}$ = $\frac{414}{25}$ **or** $16\frac{14}{25}$

27) $\frac{34}{7}$ ÷ $\frac{32}{7}$ = $\frac{17}{16}$ **or** $1\frac{1}{16}$

28) $\frac{5}{7}$ x $\frac{8}{7}$ = $\frac{40}{49}$

29) $\frac{13}{9}$ x $\frac{35}{9}$ = $\frac{455}{81}$ **or** $5\frac{50}{81}$

30) $\frac{26}{6}$ ÷ $\frac{1}{6}$ = **26**

1) $\frac{24}{6} \div \frac{14}{6} = \frac{12}{7}$ **or** $1\frac{5}{7}$

2) $\frac{5}{3} \times \frac{10}{3} = \frac{50}{9}$ **or** $5\frac{5}{9}$

3) $\frac{23}{10} \times \frac{14}{10} = \frac{161}{50}$ **or** $3\frac{11}{50}$

4) $\frac{15}{4} \div \frac{14}{4} = \frac{15}{14}$ **or** $1\frac{1}{14}$

5) $\frac{1}{4} \times \frac{14}{4} = \frac{7}{8}$

6) $\frac{21}{10} \div \frac{3}{10} = \mathbf{7}$

7) $\frac{17}{6} \div \frac{10}{6} = \frac{17}{10}$ **or** $1\frac{7}{10}$

8) $\frac{6}{4} \times \frac{13}{4} = \frac{39}{8}$ **or** $4\frac{7}{8}$

9) $\frac{21}{5} \div \frac{19}{5} = \frac{21}{19}$ **or** $1\frac{2}{19}$

10) $\frac{5}{2} \div \frac{5}{2} = \mathbf{1}$

11) $\frac{1}{5} \times \frac{15}{5} = \frac{3}{5}$

12) $\frac{7}{2} \times \frac{8}{2} = \mathbf{14}$

13) $\frac{8}{3} \div \frac{9}{3} = \frac{8}{9}$

14) $\frac{4}{6} \times \frac{23}{6} = \frac{23}{9}$ **or** $2\frac{5}{9}$

15) $\frac{8}{6} \times \frac{24}{6} = \frac{16}{3}$ **or** $5\frac{1}{3}$

58/62

16) $\frac{9}{9} \div \frac{39}{9} = \frac{3}{13}$

17) $\frac{7}{4} \div \frac{6}{4} = \frac{7}{6}$ **or** $1\frac{1}{6}$

18) $\frac{5}{10} \times \frac{48}{10} = \frac{12}{5}$ **or** $2\frac{2}{5}$

19) $\frac{18}{4} \div \frac{14}{4} = \frac{9}{7}$ **or** $1\frac{2}{7}$

20) $\frac{7}{4} \times \frac{15}{4} = \frac{105}{16}$ **or** $6\frac{9}{16}$

21) $\frac{27}{9} \div \frac{14}{9} = \frac{27}{14}$ **or** $1\frac{13}{14}$

22) $\frac{34}{7} \div \frac{4}{7} = \frac{17}{2}$ **or** $8\frac{1}{2}$

23) $\frac{14}{4} \times \frac{13}{4} = \frac{91}{8}$ **or** $11\frac{3}{8}$

24) $\frac{9}{10} \times \frac{35}{10} = \frac{63}{20}$ **or** $3\frac{3}{20}$

25) $\frac{3}{2} \times \frac{2}{2} = \frac{3}{2}$ **or** $1\frac{1}{2}$

26) $\frac{8}{7} \div \frac{31}{7} = \frac{8}{31}$

27) $\frac{4}{8} \times \frac{29}{8} = \frac{29}{16}$ **or** $1\frac{13}{16}$

28) $\frac{2}{3} \div \frac{2}{3} = \mathbf{1}$

29) $\frac{4}{6} \div \frac{26}{6} = \frac{2}{13}$

30) $\frac{7}{9} \times \frac{12}{9} = \frac{28}{27}$ **or** $1\frac{1}{27}$

1) $\frac{10}{4} \div \frac{16}{4} = \frac{5}{8}$

2) $\frac{19}{6} \times \frac{2}{6} = \frac{19}{18}$ **or** $1\frac{1}{18}$

3) $\frac{3}{3} \times \frac{7}{3} = \frac{7}{3}$ **or** $2\frac{1}{3}$

4) $\frac{25}{5} \div \frac{18}{5} = \frac{25}{18}$ **or** $1\frac{7}{18}$

5) $\frac{11}{4} \div \frac{10}{4} = \frac{11}{10}$ **or** $1\frac{1}{10}$

6) $\frac{36}{8} \div \frac{25}{8} = \frac{36}{25}$ **or** $1\frac{11}{25}$

7) $\frac{22}{5} \times \frac{18}{5} = \frac{396}{25}$ **or** $15\frac{21}{25}$

8) $\frac{27}{9} \times \frac{5}{9} = \frac{5}{3}$ **or** $1\frac{2}{3}$

9) $\frac{15}{5} \times \frac{12}{5} = \frac{36}{5}$ **or** $7\frac{1}{5}$

10) $\frac{21}{4} \div \frac{17}{4} = \frac{21}{17}$ **or** $1\frac{4}{17}$

11) $\frac{4}{6} \times \frac{2}{6} = \frac{2}{9}$

12) $\frac{27}{8} \div \frac{3}{8} = $ **9**

13) $\frac{24}{8} \div \frac{33}{8} = \frac{8}{11}$

14) $\frac{1}{2} \times \frac{1}{2} = \frac{1}{4}$

15) $\frac{4}{2} \div \frac{3}{2} = \frac{4}{3}$ **or** $1\frac{1}{3}$

59/62

16) $\frac{31}{6} \times \frac{7}{6} = \frac{217}{36}$ **or** $6\frac{1}{36}$

17) $\frac{8}{2} \times \frac{5}{2} = $ **10**

18) $\frac{30}{9} \div \frac{19}{9} = \frac{30}{19}$ **or** $1\frac{11}{19}$

19) $\frac{11}{4} \times \frac{20}{4} = \frac{55}{4}$ **or** $13\frac{3}{4}$

20) $\frac{14}{3} \div \frac{5}{3} = \frac{14}{5}$ **or** $2\frac{4}{5}$

21) $\frac{5}{2} \div \frac{11}{2} = \frac{5}{11}$

22) $\frac{23}{6} \times \frac{4}{6} = \frac{23}{9}$ **or** $2\frac{5}{9}$

23) $\frac{36}{9} \times \frac{16}{9} = \frac{64}{9}$ **or** $7\frac{1}{9}$

24) $\frac{20}{10} \div \frac{4}{10} = $ **5**

25) $\frac{1}{2} \times \frac{7}{2} = \frac{7}{4}$ **or** $1\frac{3}{4}$

26) $\frac{30}{10} \times \frac{45}{10} = \frac{27}{2}$ **or** $13\frac{1}{2}$

27) $\frac{9}{3} \div \frac{1}{3} = $ **9**

28) $\frac{10}{8} \div \frac{2}{8} = $ **5**

29) $\frac{1}{2} \div \frac{7}{2} = \frac{1}{7}$

30) $\frac{6}{8} \times \frac{1}{8} = \frac{3}{32}$

1) $\frac{17}{10} \times \frac{8}{10} = \frac{34}{25}$ **or** $1\frac{9}{25}$

2) $\frac{11}{2} \times \frac{9}{2} = \frac{99}{4}$ **or** $24\frac{3}{4}$

3) $\frac{33}{9} \div \frac{8}{9} = \frac{33}{8}$ **or** $4\frac{1}{8}$

4) $\frac{22}{5} \div \frac{17}{5} = \frac{22}{17}$ **or** $1\frac{5}{17}$

5) $\frac{28}{7} \div \frac{15}{7} = \frac{28}{15}$ **or** $1\frac{13}{15}$

6) $\frac{41}{9} \times \frac{25}{9} = \frac{1025}{81}$ **or** $12\frac{53}{81}$

7) $\frac{19}{8} \div \frac{19}{8} = $ **1**

8) $\frac{23}{8} \times \frac{34}{8} = \frac{391}{32}$ **or** $12\frac{7}{32}$

9) $\frac{33}{7} \div \frac{17}{7} = \frac{33}{17}$ **or** $1\frac{16}{17}$

10) $\frac{1}{7} \times \frac{33}{7} = \frac{33}{49}$

11) $\frac{41}{10} \times \frac{42}{10} = \frac{861}{50}$ **or** $17\frac{11}{50}$

12) $\frac{8}{3} \div \frac{11}{3} = \frac{8}{11}$

13) $\frac{5}{10} \div \frac{21}{10} = \frac{5}{21}$

14) $\frac{20}{7} \times \frac{10}{7} = \frac{200}{49}$ **or** $4\frac{4}{49}$

15) $\frac{21}{10} \times \frac{30}{10} = \frac{63}{10}$ **or** $6\frac{3}{10}$

60/62

16) $\frac{12}{4} \div \frac{7}{4} = \frac{12}{7}$ **or** $1\frac{5}{7}$

17) $\frac{17}{4} \div \frac{20}{4} = \frac{17}{20}$

18) $\frac{13}{3} \times \frac{10}{3} = \frac{130}{9}$ **or** $14\frac{4}{9}$

19) $\frac{13}{7} \times \frac{15}{7} = \frac{195}{49}$ **or** $3\frac{48}{49}$

20) $\frac{20}{10} \div \frac{31}{10} = \frac{20}{31}$

21) $\frac{20}{8} \div \frac{30}{8} = \frac{2}{3}$

22) $\frac{14}{6} \times \frac{1}{6} = \frac{7}{18}$

23) $\frac{11}{5} \times \frac{11}{5} = \frac{121}{25}$ **or** $4\frac{21}{25}$

24) $\frac{5}{2} \div \frac{5}{2} = $ **1**

25) $\frac{5}{3} \div \frac{11}{3} = \frac{5}{11}$

26) $\frac{5}{5} \times \frac{24}{5} = \frac{24}{5}$ **or** $4\frac{4}{5}$

27) $\frac{2}{4} \times \frac{17}{4} = \frac{17}{8}$ **or** $2\frac{1}{8}$

28) $\frac{5}{2} \div \frac{3}{2} = \frac{5}{3}$ **or** $1\frac{2}{3}$

29) $\frac{19}{8} \div \frac{40}{8} = \frac{19}{40}$

30) $\frac{28}{8} \div \frac{10}{8} = \frac{14}{5}$ **or** $2\frac{4}{5}$